WHO DO PEOPLE SAY I AM?

The Interpretation of Jesus In the New Testament Gospels

by
MARVIN W. MEYER

GRAND RAPIDS, MICHIGAN
WILLIAM B. EERDMANS PUBLISHING COMPANY

To Stephen and Jonathan

11/06

Copyright © 1983 by William B. Eerdmans Publishing Company
255 Jefferson Ave. S.E., Grand Rapids, MI 49503

Reprinted, December 1983

Library of Congress Cataloging in Publication Data

Meyer, Marvin W.
    Who do people say I am?
    Includes bibliographical references. + index of ancient sources
      1. Jesus Christ—History of doctrines. 2. Bible.
N.T. Gospels—Theology. I. Title.
BT198.M46 1983   226'.06   82-24229
ISBN 0-8028-1961-3

vi, 89 p.

CONTENTS

ACKNOWLEDGMENTS

I would like to express my gratitude to several people who have facilitated the production of this book. I am deeply indebted to my teacher, friend, and colleague Bastiaan Van Elderen, who has taught me to read the biblical text with care, appreciation, and enthusiasm. I also owe much to students I have had in classes where the subject matter of this book was discussed. If the reader senses an oral character to parts of the book, that derives from lively exchanges in the classroom, where an attempt was made to come to terms with the interpretations of Jesus in the New Testament. Finally, I offer my most profound thanks for the patience and support of my wife and sons, the younger of whom went to press at the same time as this book.

November 1982

MARVIN W. MEYER

INTRODUCTION

This small book is meant to function as an invitation. In this book I wish to introduce the reader to the New Testament documents, and particularly the Gospels, within their historical and human contexts. The eight chapters address eight questions that emerge from a careful and comparative study of the Gospels of Mark, Matthew, Luke, and John. By considering these questions, I hope to suggest a historical approach to the Gospels that is both reasonable and exciting.

The questions have not been chosen in a haphazard way. While at face value some of them may appear to be queries about minutia in the Gospel accounts, the questions all have been selected because of their provocative and suggestive character. They are provocative in that they present problems to the student of the New Testament, difficulties that must be taken seriously and analyzed fairly in order to comprehend the meaning of specific texts. Furthermore, these questions themselves suggest broader issues in the study of Jesus and the Gospels, and can stimulate wide-ranging discussions and reflections about the nature of the New Testament texts. The subtitles of the various chapters indicate the general issues that are at stake in each.

The arrangement of the chapters is also quite deliberate. The eight essays follow the order in which the questions appear in the Gospels, and hence move from a consideration of John the Baptist and the beginning of the good news to the resurrection of Christ as proclaimed at the conclusion of all the Gospels. In the process of moving through one chapter to the next, I trace certain themes, such as the place of the kingdom of God in the ministry of Jesus, as these themes are interpreted in the four Gospels. The development of thought is essentially inductive. Individual discussions are presented seriatim, and each chapter is intended to contribute to an overall understanding of the historical figure of Jesus and the main issues in the Gospels. Finally, at the conclusion of each chapter is a brief bibliographical comment, with suggestions for additional study.

*   *   *

In Mark 8:27–30 (cf. Matt. 16:13–20; Luke 9:18–21) we read the account of the significant happenings near Caesarea Philippi. While he was on the road, Mark narrates, Jesus asked his disciples the probing question, "Who do people say I am?" The variety of responses to this question may help us understand something about Jesus as well as about the Gospels. On the one hand, the sympathizers around Jesus explained his role in several different ways. Some said that he was filled with the spirit of John the Baptist, others that he assumed the position of Elijah, still others that he was a prophet or even the Messiah (Mark 8:28–29). So also it is with the New Testament Gospels. The evangelists respond to the inquiry about Jesus' identity with their own unique explanations and emphases. Just how each one reports and interprets the elusive, compelling presence of Jesus is the focus of this book.

The literature on the New Testament, and in particular on the New Testament Gospels, is vast, so that even getting a grasp of the basic bibliography is an overwhelming chore. Fortunately for us all, a fine professional bibliographer, David M. Scholer, has published a handy booklet entitled *A Basic Bibliographic Guide for New Testament Exegesis* (Grand Rapids: Eerdmans, 1973). This annotated *Guide* may be consulted for further reading. A more recent bibliographical publication, specifically geared to the study of the historical Jesus and the Gospels, is by David C. Aune, *Jesus and the Synoptic Gospels: A Bibliographical Study Guide* (Downers Grove: Inter-Varsity Press, 1980). Also valuable is the work by Hans Conzelmann, *Jesus* (Philadelphia: Fortress, 1973), with extensive bibliography given especially on pp. 97–116.

Quotations from the Bible (including the Old Testament apocrypha) are usually given from the Revised Standard Version, although occasionally I have modified the translation slightly. Without a doubt the most helpful edition of the Revised Standard Version is *The New Oxford Annotated Bible with the Apocrypha* (New York: Oxford Univ. Press, 1977), with extensive notes and other aids for the study of the Bible.

One monograph on the historical Jesus is probably more readable and influential than any other. That one book is the work by Günther Bornkamm, *Jesus of Nazareth* (New York: Harper & Row, 1960). Another work of enormous interest and importance is by the theologian, musician, and medical doctor Albert Schweitzer, *The Quest of the Historical Jesus* (New York: Macmillan, 1968).

1

WAS JOHN THE BAPTIST ELIJAH?

The beginning of the gospel

THE New Testament Gospels are clear in their understanding of the beginning of the ministry of Jesus of Nazareth. Once a carpenter (Mark 6:3) like his father Joseph (Matt. 13:55), Jesus turned to a second vocation when he joined up with the John the Baptist movement by being initiated through a symbolic washing, or baptism. Such an initiatory lustration was by no means rare in the ancient world, and many a devotee of this deity or that could be washed with water as a way of emphasizing the need for physical and spiritual purity before the divine. In fact, not far from where John the Baptist himself was preaching in the Judean desert, there was a Jewish baptizing commune on the Dead Sea, at Qumran, where strictly observant Jews like the Baptist gathered to make a new covenant together and to usher in the new age. Unlike these "covenanters" of Qumran, however, John apparently was part of no community, but rather was a free-lance baptizer who sought to attract Jewish followers like Jesus to a rigorous and austere life of repentance in the face of the coming kingdom (cf. Matt. 3:1–10; Luke 3:1–14).

Such is "the beginning of the gospel," the *euangelion* or good news, according to the Gospel of Mark (1:1). But the New Testament Gospels, with their concern for John the Baptist, do not constitute the earliest Christian witness to the meaning of the good news. The Gospel of Mark was written around the year 70— that is to say, around the traumatic time of the Jewish revolt and the eventual destruction of the second Jewish Temple; and the other New Testament Gospels were written somewhat later, nearer the end of the first century. But already twenty years before Mark was penned, Paul was active as a missionary and letter-writer, and he proclaimed his own authoritative yet distinctive interpretation of the gospel (e.g., Gal. 1:6–12).

When we examine the content of Paul's gospel, we find no particular interest whatsoever in the teachings or activities of the

historical Jesus, and the figure of John the Baptist is totally ig-
nored. As Paul asserts to the Corinthians, "we preach Christ crucified" (1 Cor. 1:23), and this bare datum designates his gospel.
Again and again he indicates that his proclamation is directed
toward the one who died and arose, but the precise details of the
death and resurrection of this Jesus are of little real concern to
Paul. In 1 Corinthians, however, we find one of the very first
creeds of Christendom, the Pauline creed (actually Paul claims in
1 Cor. 15:3 that he was not the author of this creed, but learned
it during his Christian "theological education," so that the creed
in its original form must antedate even Paul). We confess, says
Paul,

> that Christ died for our sins
> in accordance with the scriptures,
> that he was buried,

> that he was raised on the third day
> in accordance with the scriptures,
> and that he appeared,

at which point a list of witnesses is appended, beginning with
Cephas (Aramaic for Peter; both names mean "Rock") and culminating, naturally enough, with Paul. As my visual way of outlin-
ing the creed suggests, two confessional items stand out in this
summation of Paul's gospel: Christ died, Christ was raised. For
Paul those professions, in their stark simplicity, define the Christian gospel and the Christian faith.

The development from Paul, with his emphasis on the cross
and resurrection sketched in the broadest and boldest of strokes,
to the New Testament Gospels, with their concern for proclaiming the details of something like a "life of Jesus," took place over
only a couple of decades, but the differences in these approaches
obviously are profound. Yet, although we might find it easy to
belabor such clear differences, one factor remains constant in
Paul and the evangelists: his epistles and their Gospels point to
Jesus' passion and resurrection as the culmination of his career.
While Paul, as we have seen, asserts little more than the fact of
such a death and resurrection (what little more he does assert
about the resurrection will occupy our attention in a later chapter), the Gospels incorporate painfully explicit passion narratives
that accomplish a couple of purposes. First of all, they dwell upon
the awful specifics involved in the crucifixion of Jesus, and so

produce a running narrative on the passion. Second, they relate this passion proclamation in a self-conscious fashion to the soulful cries and prophecies of such Old Testament texts as Psalm 22, where the poet cries out, "My God, my God, why have you forsaken me?" and complains about the violent tactics of the wicked. In this manner the passion of Jesus is shown to be, from start to finish, within the prophetic plan of God.

So central is the passion story of Jesus to the New Testament Gospels that it is not an exaggeration to say that the passion and the resurrection are what these writings are all about. The life of Jesus is directed toward the cross in all four of the Gospels, throughout which the evangelists have provided hints of the bittersweet end to the story. We might pause momentarily to recall one such hint, in Luke 2:35, where old Simeon holds baby Jesus and tells Mary about a sword that will slash her soul—the cutting pain of one whose son is killed. One witty theologian, reflecting upon this centrality of the cross in the Gospels, has offered a nicely phrased definition of a New Testament Gospel that takes into account this basic focus. A Gospel, he said, is a passion story with a long introduction. The Gospels, like Paul's proclamation, weave their accounts around the cross and resurrection, but now the texture of the narrative pattern is made more variegated by means of the details of the passion narrative, set as it is within the fabric of the life of Jesus.

Our brief perambulations through the New Testament bring us back once again to John the Baptist—for the Gospels, beginning with Mark, posit that this "long introduction" to the passion story commences with the figure of the Baptist. In Mark, after the opening title (1:1) and the quotation from Isaiah, John the Baptist enters the picture, and with him, Jesus. The situation is similar in the other, later New Testament Gospels (cf. Matt. 3; Luke 3; John 1), where John's ministry precedes Jesus'. Yet, although Matthew and Luke write after Mark and apparently base their accounts on the proclaimed life of Jesus found in his Gospel, they modify Mark and add more materials to his account. That is to say, the Gospels of Matthew and Luke are careful revisions of Mark, or recast editions of that earlier Gospel. One type of material added to these Gospels has to do with the birth of Jesus. Before their reflections on John the Baptist, both Matthew and Luke add chapters on the birth of Jesus, and Luke even adds one isolated account (3:41–51) of twelve-year-old Jesus in the Temple. John, the last New Testament Gospel to be published, adds no account of Jesus' birth, but instead commences his story of Jesus by going back far beyond a birth to the place of the divine Word at creation itself (1:1–3).

In sum, the New Testament provides several options for "the beginning of the good news." Paul stresses the cross and resurrection. So do the Gospels, but Mark claims that the story of Jesus really starts with the Baptist, while Matthew and Luke preface all this with birth narratives, and John says that the proclamation of Jesus goes way back to the very beginning of creation!

Incidentally, as we trace the development of Gospel traditions, we note that in the juxtaposition of materials within the Gospels long periods of time in the life of Jesus—indeed, most of the years of his life—are not accounted for. From the time of his birth until his meeting with the Baptist, a period of around thirty years, little is described in the Bible except for the single account noted in Luke 3 of Jesus in the Temple. Nature abhors a vacuum, and so do some religious folks. Early on in the Christian movement such pious believers began to fill this vacuum by telling stories of what Jesus did during his first twelve years, incorporating these tales into what are termed "infancy gospels." Pious, sometimes bizarre, and occasionally even vicious, these apocryphal infancy gospels depict a bionic boy who performs feats of magic in the sandbox and becomes, literally, a holy terror to his teachers and friends. In these texts little Jesus stretches wooden planks for his father, baffles his teachers with his extraordinary wisdom, curses his playmates when they bother him, and makes clay sparrows fly away. The popularity of such fantastic stories is indicated not only by the number of infancy gospels that have survived from ancient times, but also by the appearance of the account of the clay birds in the Quran (*sura* 5)—even among Muhammad's Christian acquaintances this story was known! As for the following eighteen years of Jesus' life, it has remained for more contemporary minds to wax eloquent, though in candor it must be admitted that far more wax than eloquence has been produced. Silly books and documentary films have attempted to show that Jesus, during these eighteen formative but "lost" years, was jet-setting about the ancient world, from India to Egypt, in order to pick up the wisdom of the ages and the sages.

*   *   *

The relationship between John the Baptist and Jesus as portrayed in the New Testament Gospels is certainly close. For a period of time, we are told, Jesus associated with this dynamic preacher who dressed in a hair shirt, ate honey and insects, and functioned as a harsh critic of the mainline Jewish schools of the Pharisees and Sadducees (Matt. 3:4–10; Luke 3:7–14). Furthermore, according to certain ancient texts (though they are not always the most reliable texts) Jesus was not the only prominent personage within the Baptist movement. The authors of these texts claim that a certain Simon, dubbed the Magus or Magician, also was a disciple of John the Baptist. This Simon is none other than the infamous Simon who is introduced in Acts 8 and numerous other early Christian texts outside the New Testament, the Simon whose character was played so nastily by Jack Palance in the famous old film *The Silver Chalice*.

According to the New Testament Gospels, Jesus broke away from the John the Baptist people when John himself was arrested as a rabble-rousing menace (cf. esp. Mark 1:14 and Matt. 4:12). From this point on Jesus leads his own movement, and it comes as no real surprise to us when we observe that the Jesus movement is quite similar to that of John, and continues many of the patterns typical of the Baptist. To begin with, we may notice that the essential teaching of John according to Matthew 3:2 is "Repent, for the kingdom of heaven [Matthew's phrase for "kingdom of God"] is at hand." Now this message of repentance compares very well with a passage near the beginning of the Gospel of Mark that encapsulates the message of Jesus: "The time is fulfilled, and the kingdom of God is at hand; repent, and believe in the gospel" (1:15). In Matthew 4:17, the passage that is parallel to Mark 1:15, the similarity between the basic messages of John and Jesus reaches an identity. After the incarceration of John, says Matthew, Jesus begins to preach, saying, "Repent, for the kingdom of heaven is at hand." And this message of Jesus is also the same as the message proclaimed by his disciples when he sends them out on their mission (Matt. 10:7; Luke 10:9, 11).

Yet, in spite of such affinities, Jesus' ministry was unique in several ways, too. Though he gathered disciples (the Gospels list twelve in particular, probably as an anticipation of the reconstituted tribes of Israel) and taught this inner circle in an intimate fashion, as John had also done (cf. Luke 11:1, on the prayers of John and Jesus), the disciples of Jesus together with their master lived in a different manner from the severe, ascetic ways of the Baptist. For one thing, the Jesus movement was centered in Galilee, that area to the north which had the reputation of being a hotbed of political revolution and a center of incorrect Jewish observance, and not in Judea, the region around Jerusalem, where the Baptist movement was located originally. Jesus and his disciples also departed from the conduct of John the Baptist with regard to life-style. John and his people expressed their renunciation of the world by fastings and abstinences, so that some said John was out of his mind, a man possessed (Matt. 11:18; Luke 7:33). Jesus and his followers, on the other hand, did not trouble themselves with such scrupulous observances (Mark 2:18; Matt. 9:14; Luke 5:33), so that some observers accused him of eating too much, drinking too much, and associating with all the seediest sorts of people (Matt. 11:18–19; Luke 7:33–34).

The evaluation of the person of John the Baptist in the New Testament is, in general, very positive. To be sure, he plays a secondary role to that of Jesus. The Christian authors of the Gospels interpreted his role as that of forerunner, of one who prepares the way and points the way for Jesus. Even so, the Synoptic Gospels (Mark, Matthew, and Luke are termed "Synoptic" because they see Jesus in roughly the same light, since they are literarily related to each other) are particularly complimentary to John (cf. esp. Matt. 11:9–11 and Luke 7:26–28).

Without a doubt most fascinating of all the compliments paid to John is the claim, put on the lips of Jesus in Matthew, that this character, the Baptist, actually is Elijah (Matt. 11:14; 17:10–13; cf., to a lesser extent, Mark 9:11–13 and Luke 1:17)! As Matthew 11:14–15 has it, with carefully chosen words, Jesus says to the people, "If you are willing to accept it, he [that is, John] is Elijah who is to come. Whoever has ears to hear, let that person hear." The description of Elijah as one "who is to come" provides an important clue concerning the identity of this enigmatic Elijah, and the opening protasis ("If you are willing to accept it") and the closing standard plea to pay close attention ("Whoever has ears to hear . . .") alert us to the subtlety and controversy of this explanation that John the Baptist is Elijah.

Who is the "Elijah who is to come"? We may begin to appreciate the grandeur of the figure of Elijah in biblical tradition by first harking back to the "Elijah who went away." After all, Elijah is one of those marvelous Old Testament figures who is described as not passing through an ordinary death experience, but instead being miraculously translated to the heavenly realm. Elijah was swept off his feet by a whirlwind accompanied by horses and a chariot of fire (2 Kings 2:11–12), and thus he avoided a mortal end of life as we experience it. If such was the way he went from the earth, the people of Israel were convinced that he was the ideal nominee to come back to the earth again in an equally miraculous manner. This is precisely what is prophesied in Malachi 4:5, where the prophet utters a word of the Lord about Elijah returning to earth just before the Day of the Lord, when the new world order is to be ushered in: "Behold, I will send you Elijah the prophet before the great and terrible Day of the Lord comes."

If this constitutes "Elijah who is to come," it stands to reason that a time of eager anticipation of the dawning of the Day of the Lord and the kingdom of God would be, for Jews and Christians, the right time to look for Elijah. Indeed, such was—and is—the case. Apparently some of Jesus' contemporaries even suggested that he himself might be this Elijah (Mark 6:15; 8:28; Matt. 16:14; Luke 9:8, 19). Furthermore, in the transfiguration accounts (Mark 9:2–8; Matt. 17:1–8; Luke 9:28–36), who is it that can share with the glorious Christ the mountain-top experience of fantastic heavenly light? Elijah, of course, and Moses, another Old Testament hero whose death occurred under mysterious circumstances (Deut. 34:6). Lastly, to this day a prominent part of the Seder meal, the focal point of Jewish Passover celebration, includes a special cup of wine for Elijah as a celebration of hope for the people of Israel.

According to traditions in the Synoptic Gospels, then, John the Baptist was Elijah, the prophet sent to usher in the messianic age. But as we turn from the Synoptics to the Gospel of John, we find a very different evaluation of the Baptist. In the fourth Gospel John the Baptist denies that he is Elijah at all! He explicitly repudiates being the Messiah, the prophet—or Elijah (John 1:21, 25). In fact, throughout the opening chapters of John, the evangelist seemingly goes out of his way to demote the Baptist. While Jesus must increase, says the Baptist, "I must decrease" (3:30). On two occasions the evangelist even interrupts the poetic flow of his beautiful hymn to the Word with parenthetical insertions (1:6–8, 15) in order to emphasize that John is not the heavenly light and is not first in rank. For John the evangelist, then, John the Baptist was not Elijah.

In order to understand why the Baptist's rank is downgraded in the Gospel of John, we do well to consider the few bits of relevant evidence from the Acts of the Apostles. There it is stated a couple of times (18:25; 19:3–4) that Paul in his missionary endeavors in the middle portion of the century was still encountering people who had been baptized in the initiatory rite of the Baptist. The John the Baptist movement evidently did not end with the death of its founder, but continued on as a rival movement to the early Christians. One ancient text notes that some within the Baptist movement even claimed John to be the Messiah (that is, the Christ) instead of Jesus! As a matter of fact, in one way of judging the situation, the John the Baptist movement may survive to this very day among the few thousand remaining Mandaeans (or Gnostics; "Manda" means *gnosis* or knowledge) of Iraq, who claim to derive from the followers of the Baptist. In their holy book, the *Ginza*, it is Christianity that is treated as the competition, and it is Christianity that receives harsh criticism. There Jesus is depicted as one who perverts the law and encourages sorcery and error by departing from the true ways of John the Baptist. In the words of the *Ginza*, which, we readily see, could be termed an antigospel, "Jesus Christ comes, moves about in humility, is baptized with the baptism of John, and becomes wise through John's wisdom. He then proceeds to pervert the word of John and change the baptism of Jordan, altering the words of truth, and summoning wickedness and falsehood into the world." So it goes among rival religious groups and their polemics.

Was, then, John the Baptist Elijah? Yes and no, depending on the theological or polemical point of view of the biblical author. For the New Testament evangelists were involved in religious rivalries and controversies no less than any other leaders in the history of the church. These evangelists, too, like all Christian thinkers after them, were called upon to respond sensibly and thoughtfully to the burning issues of their day.

For additional analysis of John the Baptist and the kindred community at Qumran, see the brief essays in the excellent set of volumes entitled *The Interpreter's Dictionary of the Bible* (Nashville: Abingdon, 1962, 1976), 4 vols. plus Supplementary Volume. Of the several English translations of the major texts from the Dead Sea Scrolls, probably the most reliable and accessible is Geza Vermes, *The Dead Sea Scrolls in English* (New York: Penguin, 1975). Examples taken from the religions of the world of the use of sacred water in baptisms and lustrations are collected in Mircea Eliade, *Patterns in Comparative Religion* (New York: Meridian, 1963), pp. 188–215.

Discussions and translations of such infancy gospels as the Infancy Gospel of Thomas, the Gospel of (Pseudo-)Matthew, and the Gospel (Protevangelium) of James may be found in Edgar Hennecke and Wilhelm Schneemelcher, *New Testament Apocrypha* (Philadelphia: Westminster, 1963, 1965), vol. 1; and David R. Cartlidge and David L. Dungan, *Documents for the Study of the Gospels* (Philadelphia: Fortress, 1980).

Sources relating to Simon Magus, the Mandaeans, and Gnostic texts are published in Werner Foerster, *Gnosis* (Oxford: Clarendon, 1972, 1974); the quotation from the *Ginza* (trans. Kurt Rudolph) is taken from vol. 2 of this sourcebook. For helpful introductions to Simon and the Mandaeans, see Hans Jonas, *The Gnostic Religion* (Boston: Beacon, 1963); and Kurt Rudolph, *Mandaeism* (Leiden: Brill, 1978), with numerous illustrations.

Geza Vermes, *Jesus the Jew* (Philadelphia: Fortress, 1981), contains a fine discussion on Jesus as a Galilean figure, and the character of Galilee.

2

WHERE DID JESUS PREACH HIS SERMON ON THE MOUNT?

Jesus as teacher in the Gospels

A short time ago a friend was singing in a church presentation of the rock musical *Godspell*, and my wife and I were in attendance. Beginning, appropriately, with the song of the Baptist, "Prepare ye the way of the Lord," the production moved at a fast pace through a number of songs and dances, with clever and lively interpretations of the life of Jesus in a contemporary idiom. Yet what impressed me more than anything else about the musical was the lingering image of Jesus as a teacher of his disciples and acquaintances. Dressed in the attire of a clown, painted with the make-up of irenic innocence, and representative of the ideals of a modern-day urban youth culture, the Jesus of *Godspell* disseminates his teachings in familiar if reformulated sayings and parables.

For *Godspell*'s Jesus to present himself first and foremost as a teacher can be understood when we recall the purpose of the musical. *Godspell* interprets, musically and choreographically, the Gospel of Matthew; and the Gospel of Matthew, along with the Gospel of Luke, emphasizes to a considerable extent the role of Jesus as teacher. It is in the Gospel of Matthew that Jesus preaches his memorable Sermon on the Mount, to which we shall turn later in this chapter. Assuredly, the New Testament Gospels are unanimous in bearing witness to the teaching ministry of Jesus, but the Gospels of John and Mark do so in a manner quite unlike that of Matthew and Luke.

To these four approaches to Jesus as teacher we briefly turn.

*   *   *

The Gospel of John portrays Jesus teaching in a fashion remarkably different than that of Jesus in the Synoptics. If the Jesus of Mark, Matthew, and Luke speaks in concise and witty sayings, and expresses himself with one-liners that make listeners stop in their tracks, the Johannine Jesus prefers to communicate in long, sometimes rambling, and often mystical discourses about himself. Commonly these discourses are introduced with an "I am" self-predication (for instance, "I am the good shepherd," or "I am the way, and the truth, and the life"), and a literate person in the ancient world would realize the significance of such a form of expression. "I am" statements are loaded statements. Packed with revelatory connotations, these self-predications function as literary devices for an author to depict a divine personage expressing himself or herself. Thus in the Old Testament, God gives revelations in the form of self-predications (cf. Exod. 3:14; 20:2); and Isis, Harpocrates, and numerous other deities from the Mediterranean basin are also portrayed in ancient texts speaking in an "I am" fashion. For an early reader of the Gospel of John to hear Jesus speaking in precisely this manner would prompt an immediate recognition that Jesus is to be understood as an exalted, divine being uttering revelatory teachings. This recognition would suit well the vision and faith of the author of John: his Christology is high, and the Jesus he proclaims is clearly divine (e.g., John 1:1–18, the hymn to the divine Word; and 10:30, "I and the Father are one"). At the same time, John's more stylized and interpretive presentation of Jesus as divine teacher appears so theologically colored that today most New Testament scholars would rather look to the Synoptics for hints about the teachings of the historical Jesus of Nazareth. To borrow a term from art history: John's beautiful Gospel is probably the most expressionistic of the New Testament Gospels.

On the other hand, the Gospel of Mark, the "mother-gospel" of the Synoptics, includes a certain amount of typically Synoptic material describing the teacher Jesus. In Mark, like Matthew and Luke, Jesus speaks in parables, aphorisms, and poignant utterances. Yet the Markan Jesus is a man of action, a miracle-worker on a whirlwind tour of Palestine. Mark's swiftly moving Gospel nearly leaves us breathless, as one incident quickly follows another, and all happens, it seems, "immediately" (a favorite word for Mark). There simply is not much leisure time for Jesus to function as teacher in the Gospel of Mark. Instead Jesus, the mighty performer of miracles, moves inexorably toward his passion and death.

It remains for Matthew and Luke, then, to stress that Jesus was a teacher and preacher. If, as I previously proposed, Matthew and Luke rework Mark by making revisions and additions, their modifications are of several sorts. Some are merely cosmetic. Luke in particular is a man of letters, and employs a more felicitous Greek style than the hurried manner of Mark. Other revisions are for theological purposes, as Matthew and Luke select and shape their literary materials in order to propose what they each value most in their understandings of Jesus' significance. Still other modifications on the part of Matthew and Luke are related to their personal research. In addition to Mark, they knew of other oral traditions and written texts about Jesus, and hence included these materials in their edited Gospels. And one of these written sources focused upon Jesus' teachings.

Scholars have surmised for some time that a collection of sayings was used by Matthew and Luke in the compilation of their Gospels. A good case for such a sayings collection was made on the basis of a comparison of the parallels existing among the Synoptic Gospels. Suffice it to say this: when Mark, Matthew, and Luke are placed side by side, they show numerous similarities. But when Matthew and Luke disagree with Mark, they frequently agree with each other, and then ordinarily in passages presenting the teachings of Jesus. Such painstaking analyses led to the conclusion that an otherwise unknown source of Jesus' sayings, called for convenience Q (from *Quelle*, German for "source"), was picked up by Matthew and Luke and added to their Gospels, in order to produce a more pedagogical Jesus.

The embarrassment of this hypothesis was the fact that, as far as anyone knew, Q did not exist, except insofar as it could be reconstructed and reified through a careful scrutiny of Matthew and Luke. Nor was anything generically quite like Q known. The situation, in short, seemed reminiscent of the emperor's new clothes.

All of this, I am pleased to say, has changed dramatically in recent years. With the discovery of the Nag Hammadi library in 1945 and the subsequent publication of these ancient texts, a document like Q has now been located. Entitled the Gospel of Thomas, this Coptic collection of Jesus' sayings may now be related to a few small Greek fragments from Oxyrhynchus that have been known for years but have perplexed students of early Christianity. To be sure, the Gospel of Thomas should not be confused with Q. I prefer to term this Gospel a left-wing version of Q, because of its more mystical, gnosticizing tendencies. But the Gospel of Thomas, as a collection of "secret sayings" of Jesus presented one after another with no narrative structure, has vindicated the proponents of Q: here at last is an extant ancient text similar in genre and content to the hypothetical Q. Both Thomas and Q are Christian texts written by believers for whom Jesus was of chief importance as a narrator of sayings and a teacher of wisdom.

*   *   *

If the New Testament Gospels vary in their presentations, interpretations, and evaluations of the teaching ministry of Jesus, there is nonetheless no doubt but that the historical Jesus of Nazareth was a Jewish teacher and preacher in Galilee. In fact, several times in the New Testament Jesus is called "Rabbi" (e.g., Mark 9:5; 10:51; 11:21; 14:45). While there is no evidence that Jesus received any formal training in a rabbinical school, he functioned as a more informal, itinerant rabbi, and was recognized by some as an authority who could be consulted. In a number of ways Rabbi Jesus assumes typical rabbinical roles. He teaches in the synagogue on the Sabbath (Mark 1:21–28; Luke 4:31–37; Mark 6:1–6; Matt. 13:54–58; Luke 4:16–30), he gathers students and disciples around him, and of course he enters into disputes about the interpretation and observance of Torah ("Law," literally "Instruction") on such issues as the Sabbath (see Mark 2:23–28 and parallels) and divorce (see Mark 10:2–12 and parallels).

One instance of particular interest concerning Jesus as interpreter of Torah is recounted in Mark 12:28–34. When Jesus is asked about the most important commandment—that is, the essence of Torah—he responds by quoting two famous passages of Scripture: "Hear, O Israel: the Lord our God, the Lord is one; and you shall love the Lord your God ..." (Deut. 6:4); and "You shall love your neighbor as yourself" (Lev. 19:18). The first passage has always been a prominent text in Jewish worship. It is the *Shema* (Hebrew for "hear"), and to this day retains a key place in Jewish liturgy.

The account in Mark 12 reflects a typical scene in the life of a rabbi, and may be paralleled with a similar story in the Talmud (*Shabbath* 31a). During the first century of this era two famous sages, Rabbi Shammai and Rabbi Hillel, were both approached by a Gentile who requested them to define Judaism while he stood on one foot. Rabbi Shammai, noted for his temper, drove the impudent fellow off. Rabbi Hillel, a teacher of legendary patience, replied, "What is hateful to you do not do to your neighbor. That is the whole Torah, while the rest is commentary. Now go and learn it." As we note at once, the first and most essential portion of his reponse is nothing but a paraphrase of the same text that Rabbi Jesus used: Leviticus 19:18!

That the historical Jesus discussed Torah is clear; precisely how he related to the other Jewish thinkers discussing Torah in first-century Palestine is not always as clear. On the one hand, Jesus is seen in the Gospels interacting with representatives of the major schools of Jewish thought, and encountering Pharisees, Sadducees, even an occasional Zealot, as well as advocates of strict baptismal piety like those from the circles of John the Baptist. At times these encounters appear friendly enough. Jesus shares meals with Pharisees (Luke 7:36; 11:37; 14:1), has a follower from among the Zealots (Mark 3:18; Luke 6:15), and maintains cordial relationships with disciples of the Baptist even after Jesus has gone his own way (cf. Matt. 11:2–19; Luke 7:18–35). Yet some of the harshest words of Jesus in the Gospels are directed against the Pharisees, as he roundly accuses them of hypocrisy and nit-picking legalism.

Perhaps part of this hostility between Jesus and the Pharisees may stem from disagreements about the proper interpretation of Torah. The Pharisees were the progressives of their day. Open to theological growth and development, they strongly advocated the authority of an oral law (later codified into the Talmud) consisting of various judgments and legal interpretations that show God's will in every aspect of daily life. Though the Pharisaic position on the oral law was attacked by a number of first-century opponents, this approach to the Torah surely represents a creative and thoughtful sort of piety. God's will comes to expression not only in the grand and glorious passages of one's life, but also in the day-to-day details, the everyday occurrences, the seemingly insignificant moments.

According to these Pharisees, the Torah functions in a manner analogous to a yoke placed upon the necks of oxen. In the most positive way of thinking about such a yoke, one considers that the collared oxen are released from the slavery of aimless wandering and trampling, in order to plow a useful and true furrow. So also, it is said, the one who wears the yoke of the Torah is freed to live a properly ordered and directed life before God. In the words attributed to Rabbi Nehunia in the *Pirke Aboth* 3:5 (that is, the "Sayings [literally, "Chapters"] of the Fathers" in the Talmud), "Whoever takes upon himself the yoke of the Torah, from him the yoke of government and the yoke of worldly concerns will be removed. But whoever breaks off from himself the yoke of the Torah, upon him the yoke of government and the yoke of worldly concerns will be placed." Thus, the persons obedient to the way of Torah are the only ones unencumbered by the burdens and oppressions of this world, and liberated to live rightly before God.

In the New Testament, too, the yoke of the law is mentioned, though not in so approving a manner. In Matthew 11:28–30 the author shows Jesus inviting his listeners to come and take *his* yoke, *his* burden, so that they might find rest. While his yoke is described as easy, and his burden light, still the load to be carried brings the bearer under the ultimate weight of life and death, the burden of the cross (Matt. 10:37–39; 16:24–25; Mark 8:34–35; Luke 9:23–24; 14:26–27). In the middle of the first century Paul also picks up the image of the yoke in his debate about the place of Torah and circumcision for the Christian. Using some of the strongest language in this his most strongly worded letter, Paul in Galatians argues for justification by faith with a polemical twist of the phrase "yoke of the Torah." There Paul writes, "For freedom Christ has set us free; stand fast therefore, and do not submit again to a *yoke of slavery*" (5:1). In this way Paul deliberately uses his rhetorically fashioned statement to oppose a piety directed toward observance of Torah with its numerous commandments.

In the Babylonian Talmud (*Makkoth* 23b–24a) the character of the oral law is specified very exactly in terms of the famous 613 commandments. According to this section Rabbi Simlai said, "613 precepts were communicated to Moses, 365 negative precepts corresponding to the number of solar days in the year, and 248 positive precepts corresponding to the number of the members of the human body" (the Law thus has cosmic ramifications). To this assertion, the Talmud continues, Rabbi Hamnuna replied, "What is the authentic text for this? It is, 'Moses commanded us Torah, an inheritance of the congregation of Jacob' (Deuteronomy 33:4). 'Torah' being in letter-value equal to 611 [$T = 400$, $o = 6$, $r = 200$, $h = 5$, for a total of 611; a, being a lowly vowel-point, does not count in the numeration], and 'I am' and 'You shall have no other gods' not being reckoned because we heard them from the mouth of the Might Divine" (hence $611 + 2 = 613$ precepts, QED).

By the way, this same section of the Talmud is significant for New Testament studies for another reason. According to the succeeding paragraphs of *Makkoth*, various teachers and sages in Jewish history besides Hillel (and Jesus) have searched for the most important commandments of Torah, the essential precepts for Jewish life. David, it is claimed, suggested eleven principles (Ps. 15), Isaiah six (Isa. 33:15–16), Micah three (Micah 6:8), Isaiah, again, two (Isa. 56:1), Amos one (Amos 5:4)—and Habakkuk based all of Torah on one principle, "The righteous shall live by faith" (Hab. 2:4). Hence, according to the Jewish oral law, the whole system of Torah is established upon the very same text used by the Christian missionary Paul (cf. Gal. 3:11) to argue *against* the value of the Law for salvation!

As I have already intimated, the position of the Pharisees on the Torah did not go uncontested in the first-century Palestinian world. For example, the Sadducees, as theological conservatives, had no use for the oral law, but adhered only to the written word of God: if God didn't write it, they didn't believe it! The Christian motto *sola scriptura* could function rather well as the slogan of the Sadducees.

According to Mark 7, Rabbi Jesus may also have criticized the Pharisees for their advocacy and application of the oral law. In the context of a debate about ritual cleanness, Jesus calls the Pharisees hypocrites, and accuses them of promoting human teachings at the expense of confronting the divine word: "You leave the commandment of God, and hold fast the tradition of human beings" (7:8). This human tradition passed on in Pharisaic circles (7:13) is the oral law, and Jesus' stern words denouncing the Pharisees and their legal interpretation stress that the real concern in God's law is the human heart, the human will. In Mark, Jesus concludes by asserting that the more essential problem regarding cleanliness is not the dirt of the hands but instead the dirt of the heart. The words of Mark 7:15 express this concern in a strikingly pungent manner: "there is nothing outside people which by going into them can defile them; but the things which come out of people are what defile them."

Obviously Jesus' interpretation of Torah actually intensifies its application in human life. Mere conformity to the letter of the

16

Law does not suffice. One might be technically observant of the Sabbath, or legally proper in divorce proceedings, and yet miss the intent of the Law: love and mercy (besides Mark 2 and 10, cf. also 3:1–6). As Matthew 23:23–24 puts it (cf. Luke 11:42) in a woe uttered by Jesus, the scribes and Pharisees are careful in their observance of the ritual requirements of Torah, but they "have neglected the weightier matters of the Law, justice and mercy and faith," and so have been "straining out a gnat and swallowing a camel!" Love radically defined summarizes Jesus' words on Torah, a love that extends to one's neighbor and beyond. With his authoritative assertion, "But I say to you" (Luke 6:27–28; cf. Matt. 5:21–48), Jesus proposes such a love without limits, in the most self-giving of terms: "Love your enemies, do good to those who hate you, bless those who curse you, pray for those who abuse you"—just as God is merciful and gracious to the undeserving and the ungrateful (Luke 6:35–36)

*   *   *

In order to understand better the context within the teaching ministry of Jesus for his reflections upon the Law, we should return once again to Mark 12 and Jesus' conversation about the essence of Torah. There Jesus concludes the discussion with a telling state.nent to the scribal interlocutor: "You are not far from the kingdom of God" (12:34). With this response Jesus raises an issue that dominates his teaching more than any other concern, an issue that forms the setting within which even his interpretation of the Law finds its place. That issue is the announcement of the kingdom of God, the rule of God breaking into human history and transforming human lives. The dominant motif in the career of Jesus the teacher, as it was also of major interest within the proclamation of John the Baptist, the kingdom of God is presented as the urgent challenge to be faced by all. In the words of Mark 1:15, "The time is fulfilled, and the kingdom of God is at hand; repent, and believe in [God]" (here Mark uses his own word, "gospel," instead of "God," the sort of word that Jesus would have utilized). "The time is fulfilled": the present world order, with its values and its ills, is about to topple, overthrown by the power of God, and now is the time for repentance in the face of God's imminent judgment and redemption. The point of view of Jesus' announcement is usually termed apocalyptic, in the sense of an "unveiling" or "uncovering" of the meaning of history, of the end of one kingdom and the beginning of another. Like some of the Old Testament prophets, the book of Daniel, and several intertestamental authors, Jesus proclaims that God will intervene to usher in a new age. Moreover, there is both a present and a future reality to this intervention of God as announced by Jesus. In the exact and appropriately ambiguous language of the announcement, the kingdom is "at hand" or "near." If I may use a metaphor or two: it is dawning, it is budding, but it is not yet shining in its full glory nor vivid in its full bloom.

This tension concerning present and future dimensions of the kingdom will occupy our attention in a later chapter. Nevertheless, here I should add one further observation. Just as we resorted to metaphorical language to elucidate something of the nature of the kingdom, so also Jesus made use of the figurative language of the parable (in Hebrew, *mashal*) in his proclamation of the kingdom. Thus:

> With what can we compare the kingdom of God, or what parable shall we use for it? It is like a grain of mustard seed, which, when sown upon the ground, is the smallest of all the seeds on earth; yet when it is sown it grows up and becomes the greatest of all shrubs, and puts forth large branches, so that the birds of the air can make nests in its shade. (Mark 4:30–32)

That is, although the kingdom has an inconsequential, nearly invisible beginning with a few humble folks gathered around an unofficial rabbi in the hinterland of the Roman Empire, still the tiny beginning has been made, and one day the kingdom will flower (once more, a nearly automatic retreat to metaphor) into a mighty band of God's people. "Again, the kingdom of heaven is like a merchant in search of fine pearls, who, on finding one pearl of great value, went and sold all that he had and bought it" (Matt. 13:45–46). That is, the worth of the kingdom is so overwhelming that nothing on earth can compare with it. It is the ultimate prize that necessitates the ultimate commitment.

*   *   *

Thus far we have seen that Jesus of Nazareth was a Jewish teacher with apocalyptic interests, and that in general he is portrayed as such in the New Testament Gospels, though the evangelists vary in their specific interpretations of his teachings. But of all the images that might come to mind to capture our fancy concerning Jesus as teacher, none is as common and vivid as that scene shown in paintings, recreated in films, and highlighted in tours of Galilee—the famous spectacle of the Sermon on the Mount as presented in Matthew 5–7.

According to Matthew, Jesus goes up on a mountain, takes a seat, and teaches his followers (5:1–2). Beginning with the Beatitudes, Jesus proceeds to deliver a speech that extends for three long chapters. When we recall other long speeches of Jesus in the New Testament, we think at once of the Gospel of John. Yet the structure of Matthew's Sermon is not like the long discourses of John. Matthew's Sermon is composed of smaller units of material assembled together as a package of comments, in particular on the fulfillment of the Torah. Following the speech, the curtain descends with a concluding statement of the audience's astonishment and approval (7:28–29).

Now as we compare Matthew 5–7 with the other Synoptics, we discover that only Luke has an appreciable amount of material parallel to that in Matthew's Sermon on the Mount. This discovery might be anticipated on the basis of our previous observations concerning the Q material. What could not be anticipated, however, is that Luke puts Q to use in his Gospel in a manner quite different from Matthew. Matthew collects Q material together to form larger chunks of sermonic material like the Sermon on the Mount. Luke prefers to work Q into the unfolding account of his Gospel, leaving the sayings in smaller segments. The end result is that Matthew's Jesus delivers long sermons, while Luke's does not.

There is one important exception to this pattern. Though in Luke, Jesus delivers no Sermon on the Mount, he does utter a Sermon on the Plain (Luke 6:20–49; for the level place cf. 6:17) that includes much of the same material as Matthew's Sermon on the Mount! Both Sermons, for example, begin with the Beatitudes, and though clear differences do exist (Luke has fewer Beatitudes, is less overtly "spiritualized" about the poor and the hungry, and adds woes to the blessings), both versions proclaim a similar fundamental message: the coming of the kingdom brings a drastic reversal of fortunes for all people. In Luke, then, the Sermon on the Mount is pronounced, in a shorter form, on a plain.

As we turn back for a closer look at Matthew, we initially note that his Sermon on the Mount is only the first of several major speeches delivered by Jesus. Each of these long speeches, of which there are five, is organized around a general theme, and is concluded with a stylized formula drawing the scene to a close (e.g., Matt. 7:28–29, the end of the Sermon on the Mount). The remaining speeches are these: Matthew 10:5–42, a missionary address by Jesus to the twelve, which concludes at 11:1; 13:1–52, which contains parables of Jesus and concludes at 13:53; 18:1–35, where Jesus speaks about life together in community (18:17 even has Jesus refer, anachronistically, to "church," an obvious instance of an interest of Matthew put onto the lips of Jesus), which ends at 19:1; and finally, 24:3–25:46, in which Jesus talks about eschatology, and which is brought formally to its conclusion at 26:1.

What sort of picture of Jesus do we get from Matthew, then? Matthew's Jesus is preeminently a teacher concerned with instruction in the Law and in community life. So concerned is Matthew for his church that he has Jesus preach directly to it. Jesus offers five major blocks of instructional material, the first of which is given as a revelation on a mountain.

In other words, Matthew seems to understand Jesus to be a new Moses for a new day. Just as Moses was a lawgiver, so Jesus reveals a newly formulated Law, a Christian Torah, as Matthew might put it. As Moses ascended Mount Sinai, so Jesus went up the Galilean mountain. And as Moses authored the five books of Pentateuchal Law (Genesis–Deuteronomy), so also Jesus utters five new "books" of authoritative Torah.

Even more can be made of Jesus as a new Moses in Matthew's interpretation. For Matthew's account of the birth of Jesus (chaps. 1–2), an account fashioned quite differently from Luke's, also encourages the reader to recall Moses. The story of the Old Testament Moses includes a good Joseph, and so does the story of Jesus. The first Moses was oppressed as a baby by the wicked pharaoh, just as Matthew's "second Moses" is pursued, as an infant, by the wicked Herod. The old Moses led the people of Israel on an Exodus of liberation from Egypt, and the baby Jesus, according to Matthew, likewise experiences a new Exodus from Egypt. In case the Exodus parallel might not be obvious to one of his readers, Matthew presses the issue of his interpretation when he states in 2:15 that the return of the holy family from Egypt fulfilled a prophecy of Hosea (11:1). A quick glance at this text (as well as at Exod. 4:22) suffices to show that Hosea, and hence Matthew, are both commenting on the Exodus. As Hosea phrases it, in parallel poetic lines,

> When Israel was a child, I loved him,
> and out of Egypt I called my son.

In short, Matthew's Jesus relives, as it were, the key events in the history of Israel, in anticipation of his role as lawgiver for the church.

Thus, the precise locale of the Sermon on the Mount in the Gospel of Matthew is less a point of geographical interest than a matter of his theological agenda. Matthew's evaluation of Jesus as teacher accentuates the authoritative, revelatory nature of the instruction, and so Jesus sermonizes from a vantage point immediately reminiscent of divine potency. The closing formula of the Sermon on the Mount makes this point explicit. Jesus taught the people "as one who had authority, and not as their scribes" (7:29). Furthermore, for most people of the ancient world, a mountain was not simply a heap of stones. Rather, a mountain was the dwelling place of the gods and the source of divine disclosures. Mountains were exalted above mortal reality and hidden in clouds of mystery, and these very clouds were thought to release divine glory and the divine voice in lightning and thunder (e.g., Exod. 19:16; 20:18; Pss. 18:13–14; 77:18; 104:7). All such associations between mountains and the divine convinced people that the sacred becomes manifest on the holy mountain, whether that be Fuji, Olympus, Zion, Carmel, Sinai—or the Mountain of the Sermon. Accordingly, Matthew wants to proclaim that Jesus preached his Sermon not upon a geological configuration, but from a position of authority.

It is interesting to notice that a mountain of authority is part of Matthew's theological landscape at the climax of his Gospel, too. The last verses of Matthew picture the risen Christ, sovereign over the cosmos, as he mandates his followers to preach the kind of observance he himself revealed—and here again he is positioned upon a mountain in Galilee. Thus Matthew leaves his readers with forceful words from a risen Christ who continues to lead the church: go, baptize, teach.

Further analysis, with bibliography, of issues faced in the comparative study of the Synoptic Gospels, Q, and the Gospel of John may be found in a standard introduction to the New Testament. Two good examples of such introductions are the detailed reference book by Werner Georg Kümmel, *Introduction to the New Testament* (Nashville: Abingdon, 1975), and the more popular work by Norman Perrin and Dennis C. Duling, *The New Testament: An Introduction* (New York: Harcourt Brace Jovanovich, 1982).

For fine and concise studies on the parables and the Sermon on the Mount, see two books by Joachim Jeremias, *The Parables of Jesus* (New York: Charles Scribner's Sons, 1972), with its description of the development from the parables of Jesus to the allegorical revisions of the parables as employed by the early church; and *The Sermon on the Mount* (Philadelphia: Fortress, 1963). A reliable translation of the Gospel of Thomas is published in *The Nag Hammadi Library in English*, ed. James M. Robinson and Marvin W. Meyer (Leiden: Brill; San Francisco: Harper & Row, 1977). The best book on the infancy accounts of Matthew and Luke is by Raymond E. Brown, *The Birth of the Messiah* (Garden City: Doubleday, 1977).

Representative "I am" self-predications attributed to Isis and Harpocrates are published in Frederick C. Grant, *Hellenistic Religions* (Indianapolis: Bobbs-Merrill, 1953), pp. 128–34.

Jewish schools of thought from the time of Jesus are introduced by D. S. Russell, *Between the Testaments* (Philadelphia: Fortress, 1965), and Marcel Simon, *Jewish Sects at the Time of Jesus* (Philadelphia: Fortress, 1967). The translations from the Talmud are taken (with slight revisions) from *The Babylonian Talmud*, ed. I. Epstein (London: Soncino, 1935–52).

3

WHAT DID JESUS MEAN BY "OUR FATHER"?

The devotional language of Jesus and early Christians

CERTAINLY one of the most well-known symbols of Christendom is the prayer that has come down through history under the title "The Lord's Prayer." Many civic events and public meetings have been graced with an invocation consisting of this prayer, so that it sometimes functions, in a manner not unlike a national anthem or a pledge of allegiance, as an expression of popular piety and general values. In churches, too, the Lord's Prayer is so familiar that if any single prayer is likely to be recited aloud by the congregation, it is this prayer (though the slight variations in wording can make for moments of uncertainty; in Riverside Church in New York City, I recall, the situation is clarified in the church bulletin by means of a discreetly placed parenthetical insertion of a single word: "debts"). Throughout the entire history of the church the paradigm for prayer has usually been the "Pater noster," the Lord's Prayer.

But which Lord's Prayer? In raising this question I am not thinking merely of the slight variations just alluded to, but rather I would turn our attention to the several versions of the prayer preserved in ancient Christian literature. Besides the significant suggestions and comments included in such apocryphal documents as the Gospel of the Hebrews and the *Didache* ("The Teaching of the Lord through the Twelve Apostles," a beautiful Christian text that some church fathers wanted to include in the New Testament canon), the variant versions of the Lord's Prayer found in the New Testament Gospels of Matthew and Luke require our careful examination:

Matthew 6:9–13	*Luke* 11:2–4
Our Father who are in heaven,	
	Father,
Hallowed be your name.	Hallowed be your name.
Your kingdom come.	Your kingdom come.

23

Your will be done,
On earth as it is in heaven.
Give us this day our daily
    bread;
And forgive us our debts,
As we also have forgiven our
    debtors.

And lead us not into
    temptation,
But deliver us from evil.

Give us each day our daily
    bread;
And forgive us our sins,
For we ourselves
    forgive every one
    who is indebted to us.
And lead us not into
    temptation.

Obviously the version of the Lord's Prayer according to Matthew is the longer of the two, and the more familiar in contemporary liturgical usage. The popularity of Matthew's Prayer is quite understandable, since his more expanded passages have a pleasing style appropriate for worship in the ancient church as well as in the modern. In some manuscripts, though not the oldest, the doxology "For yours is the kingdom . . ." is added, but ordinarily these words now are relegated to a footnote in English translations. They clearly were added later by the church as a worthy conclusion to the Prayer. All of this is presented by Matthew within Jesus' Sermon on the Mount, as an example of sincerity and brevity in prayer.

In Luke the more abbreviated Lord's Prayer is delivered by Jesus in a different context. After Jesus finished praying, Luke says, a disciple asked to be instructed in prayer just like John the Baptist instructed his disciples. In response to this request Jesus provides the Lord's Prayer in the Lukan form. Following the prayer Luke concludes the scene with two additional comments of Jesus: the story of the friend's persistent, nocturnal inquiry (11:5–8), and Jesus' final statements about how God the Father answers prayer (11:9–13; Matthew includes this material a bit later in the Sermon on the Mount, at 7:7–11).

The shorter version of the Lord's Prayer in Luke presents another challenge. For if we consult the King James translation of Luke 11:2–4, we discover that there the Lukan Prayer is nearly identical with that of Matthew, except for a couple minor differences in wording (e.g., "day by day" in Luke 11:3 and "this day" in Matt. 6:11), and the omission of the doxology that the King James translators included in the Matthean Prayer (6:13). The reason for these more impressive similarities stems not from the harmonizing tendencies of this translational team back in 1611, but rather from the sorts of manuscripts the King's men had at their disposal. Their work, artful as it was, was based upon manuscripts that are not as old nor as accurate as the ancient texts we now employ for most translations of the Bible. These later manuscripts used for the King James Version show that scribes who knew the New Testament intimately were aware of the differences in older texts of the Gospels, and hence wished to "improve" Luke by bringing his Lord's Prayer into conformity with Matthew's. This modification they accomplished by adding "Our ... who are in heaven" after "Father" (more easily accomplished in Greek than in English); "Your will be done ..." after "Your kingdom come"; and "But deliver us from evil" after "And lead us not into temptation." A few of the more eager scribes went the final distance in textual harmonization by changing even those minute differences in wording to bring the two versions of the Lord's Prayer into complete agreement.

Thus, in the history of manuscript traditions we find an increasing tendency toward harmonizing discrepancies. That is, some of the later manuscripts of the New Testament edit the texts to bring a uniformity to the documents that is not present in the oldest texts. The implications of this observation are at least twofold. First, the argument occasionally articulated these days, that the earliest, original texts of the Bible (that is, the *autographa*) could have manifested flawless congruence and coherence, simply does not fit the manuscript evidence. The witness of the manuscripts is that the earliest texts provided the variety and novelty that are resolved in the synthesizing, reconciling efforts of later scribes. So, if any texts are likely to be in complete harmony, they are not the early texts, but the later ones. Second (and in particular directed toward our present discussion), we should allow the two New Testament versions of the Lord's Prayer to stand as two forms in which the Prayer was preserved by early churches and their evangelists Matthew and Luke during the latter half of the first Christian century.

Of these two versions of the Lord's Prayer, which then is the earliest? Suffice it to say that the evidence is not conclusive, but a good case can be made for Luke's shorter Prayer as the older of the two forms. Luke's version is a terse, almost abrupt prayer, and ordinarily we assume that one of the propensities that can be observed in the copying of manuscripts is the expansion and embellishment of texts. This trend is especially evident in materials used in worship, where the more elaborate and parallel structure that we observe in Matthew's Prayer would be quite appropriate for a Christian congregation at worship. We need only think of the sorts of materials used in contemporary worship to see that nicely balanced lines and rich statements of faith make for excellent congregational responses and supplications. Furthermore, the essential petitions in the two versions of the Lord's Prayer do in fact agree. Matthew differs from Luke only in that he expands the petitions with prayerful statements, bringing a heightened liturgical sense to the prayer. Thus, the Lord's Prayer as found in the Gospel of Luke probably provides us with the oldest basic form of the Prayer; but Matthew preserves very old wording too, and amplifies so well a simpler prayer that he has produced a version of the Lord's Prayer that is still in use today.

The matter of the wording of the Lord's Prayer requires an additional remark or two. To illustrate the complexities we face in dealing with the precise wording of these two forms of the Prayer, we might examine the petition in Luke regarding the forgiveness of sins. Luke has Jesus pray about sins, Matthew speaks of debts. Yet Luke concludes the petition with a reference back to "every one who is indebted to us," and thereby suggests that he may have changed an earlier wording similar to Matthew's, with its petition "forgive us our debts," to his own preferred and more general wording, "forgive us our sins." Such fine points in the texts have led one prominent scholar to conclude that the form of the Lord's Prayer as we find it in Luke is closer to the original length of the prayer, while the text as we find it in Matthew sometimes is closer to the original words and phrases.

The topic just discussed is obscured, however, in the recently published New International Version of the Bible—where it is relegated to a footnote. The translation given for Luke 11:4 is "for we also forgive everyone who sins against us." To be sure, the footnote mentions that the Greek has "everyone who is indebted to us," and the modified translation does allow for good English style in the body of the text. Yet by confining Luke's reference to indebtedness to a note, the translators have played down the significance of Luke's peculiarities of word choice, and have impeded, albeit in a minor way, the search for the oldest wording of the Lord's Prayer.

*　　　*　　　*

Perhaps nowhere else are the teachings of Jesus more profoundly summarized than in the Lord's Prayer. As we now have it, the Lord's Prayer is preserved in Greek (and the various translations from the Greek), but the original model Prayer would have been uttered by Jesus in Aramaic, his native tongue. Several scholars have undertaken the difficult task of reconstructing an Aramaic original for the Lord's Prayer from the Greek texts of Luke and Matthew, in order to approximate the prayer as it would have been spoken by those in the circle of Jesus' followers.

The Lord's Prayer is a Jewish prayer, and the elements within it can be found throughout Jewish liturgy. For example, if Jesus prayed "Father" (the Greek *Pater* translates the Aramaic *Abba*), so also is this basic form of address common in other Jewish prayers, where "Our Father" (*Abinu* in Hebrew, or *Abuna* in Aramaic) is a typical way of invoking God. Matthew's longer address is also well represented in Jewish piety, and a text like the *Pirke Aboth* 5:20 refers easily to the will of "your Father who is in heaven." If the Lord's Prayer speaks of God's name and his kingdom, so do forms of the *Kaddish* ("Holy"), a prayer used in synagogue worship: "Magnified and sanctified be his great name. . . . May he establish his kingdom during your life and during your days, and during the life of all the house of Israel, speedily and soon." If the Lord's Prayer asks for bread and forgiveness, so also the Eighteen Benedictions (*Shemoneh Esreh*) requests of God the produce and goodness of the year, and the pardon and forgiveness of transgressions. And if those using the Lord's Prayer plead for deliverance from temptation, so does the Talmudic text *Berakoth* 60b, which includes the prayer, "Do not accustom me to transgression, and bring me not into sin, or into iniquity, or into temptation, or into contempt. And may the good inclination have sway over me, and let not the evil inclination have sway over me."

Rabbi Jesus thus teaches his disciples a prayer that is characteristically Jewish, yet he presents it thematically and stylistically in a distinctive way. The petitions of the prayer go hand in hand with Jesus' proclamation of the kingdom. The first two petitions concerning God's name and kingdom belong together; in a complementary fashion they look for the vindication of God's glory

27

and God's rule. God's name is exalted, in fact, specifically in the triumph of his kingdom and in the inauguration of his new world order. The two petitions requesting bread and forgiveness for "us" likewise are directed toward the consummation of God's reign. The "daily bread" or, perhaps better, the "bread for tomorrow," is food for the present day in anticipation of the glorious banquet of the coming age (cf. Luke 22:28–30), and the forgiveness practiced now is linked to the future forgiveness and acceptance on the part of God. The additional petition for strength in the midst of temptation is an appeal for endurance in the face of trials, and especially the intense birth-pangs of the coming kingdom (cf. Mark 13:7–8, 19–20, and parallels). Consequently, all the petitions look toward the future realization of the kingdom of God that is presently being experienced in the food and forgiveness granted by God.

In terms of style the Lord's Prayer also exhibits distinctive traits. In both versions of the Prayer, and especially in Luke's form, the Lord's Prayer displays a remarkable conciseness, simplicity, and directness. No showy turns of phrase grace the prayer, no prolonged elegance delights the mouth and the ear. In contrast even to other Jewish prayers, this Prayer of Jesus is exceptional for its childlike openness in petitioning God. This is preeminently the case with the opening form of address: "Father," *Abba*.

*   *   *

The term *Abba*, "the father" (the practical equivalent of "my father" or "our father"), is employed several times in the New Testament. In Mark 14:36 Jesus' earnest prayer in Gethsemane addresses God with the word *Abba* (translated immediately thereafter by Mark with the Greek for "Father"). In Romans 8:15 and Galatians 4:6 Christian acclamations to God take the form of "*Abba*, Father!" In these three instances *Abba* is utilized uniformly in the context of prayer, in a manner quite like the Aramaic term of address uttered by Jesus and his followers in the Lord's Prayer. This intimate term comes from a familial context, and expresses the attitude of children toward their "daddy." Hence its use in prayer suggests a relationship of warmth and trust between a divine Father and his believing children.

In Judeo-Christian thought God frequently is depicted as a heavenly Father. The Bible is clear in highlighting the personal character of the divine. Not an abstract force nor an impersonal ultimate principle, God is described as a person who has a name (see Exod. 3:13–15), and who has interpersonal dealings with his people. Furthermore, he is considered a fatherly person. Israel calls to him, "My Father" (Jer. 3:4, 19), and God in turn loves his son Israel (Hos. 11:1–4), and demands of the Egyptian pharaoh that he release his son, for "Israel is my first-born son" (Exod. 4:22–23). To David God promises to bless the future King Solomon: "I will be his Father, and he shall be my son" (1 Chron. 17:13). Even in the midst of devastation God promises, "I am a Father to Israel, and Ephraim is my first-born" (Jer. 31:9), while a faithful prophet confesses, "O Lord, you are our Father" (Isa. 63:16; 64:8).

The fatherhood of God as articulated within Jewish and Christian theology may be set against the backdrop of the intellectual history of the ancient Middle East. The eastern portion of the ancient Mediterranean world often exhibited a theological system that featured, among the assemblage of deities in the pantheon, a Sky Father and an Earth Mother. (The last vestiges of the Earth Mother survive in our flippant references to Mother Nature, who lately has been revivified in television commercials featuring a divine mother wielding thunderbolts and hawking some sort of margarine.) Often the emergence of fertility upon the face of the earth—the growth of crops, the birth of babies, the rebirth of the year—was pictured as the fruition of cosmic intercourse between the sky god and the earth goddess. The rain, or semen of heaven, penetrates into the womb of the earth, impregnating the earth with life itself. Such life is the gift of the divine Father, the rider of clouds, who goes by names like Zeus, Jupiter, El, and Baal.

Now the Hebrew people encountered such religious traditions among their neighbors, and often were sorely tempted to follow their ways. The most acute struggles came when they threw off their nomadic, bedouin past, and embraced a settled, agricultural existence, with the vital need for fertile land. How were they to harness the powers of the earth, how could they sabotage the forces of death and nurture the moist soil with its promise of sustenance? Today we harness the land in part by means of organic and chemical additives. In the ancient world farmers turned with pious concern to the earth and applied what we might term "theological fertilizer," gifts and offerings of devotion to the powers of mother earth. As the Old Testament prophets make abundantly clear, the Hebrew people found the fertility cults of their neighbors to be immensely attractive, and repeatedly offered their allegiance and love to an Anath, or an Astarte, or another deity of the earth. As Hosea intones against the northern farmers of Israel,

> you have played the harlot, forsaking your God.
> You have loved a harlot's hire upon all threshing floors. (9:1)

One of the tactics directed against the apostasy of the Hebrew people was a theological one. The earth, it was proclaimed, is by no means divine. In the beginning (so asserts Gen. 1) *God* created, and all the supposedly divine forces under heaven—the waters of prince Sea (Yamm) and judge River (Nahar), the glorious heavenly bodies, and the life-giving Earth itself (or herself)—are merely creatures, things created by the one God who dwells alone as the heavenly Father.

From the perspective of the history of religions, the Lord's Prayer addressed to "Our Father" is a part of this exceedingly old tradition of the paternal deity who lives in heaven above. In some ancient traditions, as we have noted, he has a godly mate in the earth. The existence of an earthly consort of the heavenly Father, however, is vehemently denied by many Jews and Christians from antiquity, so that a monotheistic theological system with a Father God has become the common parlance of our discussions about God.

On the other hand, some Jews and Christians in ancient as well as modern times have tried to reinstate the maternal dimension of deity in a formal theological way. Refugees and recruits from Palestine, for instance, settled long ago at Elephantine Island in Egypt, built a Jewish temple there, and proceeded to worship (in addition to Yaho, or Yahweh, the Lord of Israel) the very deities that the Old Testament prophets were denouncing. One of these deities of the Egyptian Israelites was the fertility mother Anath, who may have functioned as a consort of Yaho (cf. Jer. 44 on the worship of "the queen of heaven"). Again, in Proverbs (and even more so in the intertestamental wisdom literature) the Wisdom of God is personified as the first creature of God (Prov. 8:22), his companion during creation (8:23–31), the exalted being who calls people to turn to truth and understanding (8:1–13) and who controls the destinies of the mighty people of the earth (8:14–21). Wisdom is *Hokhmah* in Hebrew and *Sophia* in Greek. Both terms are feminine in gender, and both personifications were widely used in ancient literature to represent an exalted and sometimes even divine Female. One final example of the quest for a divine mother in ancient Judeo-Christian theology: as is widely known today, and much discussed in current theological deliberations, some early Christian groups proposed that God the Holy Spirit was God the Mother, and hence described the holy Trinity as a divine nuclear family, with a Father, a Son, and also a Mother.

*   *   *

Almost 2,000 years ago Jesus and his followers prayed to God as Father, with a striking simplicity and a childlike intimacy. Today we are still moved in our use of this beautiful prayer in our own worship. In referring to God as Father, Jesus and his disciples used a traditional term, originally borrowed from human experience in the family and applied to the deity as experienced in religious life. Not that God need be considered specifically male, or representative of a particular social or familial role. Rather, an appropriate category from everyday life was adopted for expressing something about God and God's relationship with people. In this manner the first-century Palestinian context shaped the choice of descriptive terms used for God in the prayers of Jesus and his friends. "God-talk" is always like that. Formulated in human language, our "God-talk" haltingly seeks to express the ineffable in the limited context of the vocabulary with which we are conversant. It remains the constant challenge for believers to show as much creativity, sensitivity, and humility in theological formulations as was evident in the earliest church.

For an excellent little book on the Lord's Prayer, see the work by the "prominent scholar" alluded to above, Joachim Jeremias, *The Lord's Prayer* (Philadelphia: Fortress, 1964). On p. 15 Jeremias suggests his Aramaic reconstruction of the prayer. Also very helpful is the article on the Lord's Prayer in *The Interpreter's Dictionary of the Bible* (Nashville: Abingdon, 1962), 3:154–58. Of the translations of Jewish literature in this chapter, some are based upon the Soncino edition of the Babylonian Talmud, the others are taken from the fine book by the Jewish scholar C. G. Montefiore, *Rabbinic Literature and Gospel Teachings* (New York: KTAV, 1970).

James B. Pritchard, *Ancient Near Eastern Texts Relating to the Old Testament* (Princeton: Princeton Univ. Press, 1969), provides a helpful sourcebook of texts illustrating some of the motifs of fertility religion. Especially useful is the section on Baal and Anath, and their adventures with prince Yamm, judge Nahar, and finally Mot (Death) himself (Ugaritic texts, pp. 129–42). A general introduction to such religious traditions is given by Helmer Ringgren, *Religions of the Ancient Near East* (Philadelphia: Westminster, 1973).

A brief discussion about the Jewish community at Elephantine may be found in H. Idris Bell, *Cults and Creeds in Graeco-Roman Egypt* (Chicago: Ares, 1975). His chapter entitled "The Jews in Egypt" offers a good description of the pluralistic nature of Egyptian Judaism. The books and articles on Wisdom and the Holy Spirit are legion; one pleasing description is in Elaine H. Pagels, *The Gnostic Gospels* (New York: Random House, 1979), pp. 48–69, with additional references in the footnotes.

4

WAS JESUS
AN EXORCIST?

Interpreting the miracles of Jesus

FROM a medical point of view the old days were not necessarily the good old days. Before the development of modern medicine and the outstanding improvements in medical research, diagnosis, and treatment, one's health and well-being were much more fragile than they are today. We might reflect upon even relatively recent times when a slug of whiskey and a silver bullet had to suffice for anesthesia during various sorts of chilling surgical maneuvers. But in the ancient world, little real medical attention was available for a great many of the people. Frequently ordinary people had to cope with injury and disease as best they could, by making use of folk remedies and traditional cures. In villages of Upper Egypt, where the old world of the pharaohs lives on to an amazing extent, the sick, the maimed, the retarded, and the dying may still be seen lying out on the streets. Even today such individuals and their families look, often in vain, for someone to grant healing.

Within such a setting, ancient or modern, it stands to reason that people would flock to receive the cures and the relief offered by faith-healers and miracle-workers who claim to function as channels for supernatural power. A good deal of the popularity enjoyed by Jesus and others who have supposedly possessed healing abilities has stemmed from the fervent hopes of suffering people, whose only prospects for relief from their ills lie with such holy figures. As a result, to this very day healing services are often jammed with a multitude seeking to be restored, and the pillars of the centers of healing around the world are cluttered with the crutches and orthopedic paraphernalia of those who have recovered their health. So it was also in the ancient world: the infirmed masses crowded around the miracle-workers, and presented themselves at health shrines like that of the Greek god of healing, Asclepius, at Epidauros. And in the ancient world too the healers and wonder-workers received very mixed reviews for

33

their efforts. Some were applauded as "divine men and women"; others were accused of crassly looking to make a quick drachma at the expense of the gullible public.

For many a physical disease or psychological disorder the ancient diagnosis could differ substantially from a modern medical assessment. Commonly it was concluded that an evil force of some sort possessed a patient, and worked its vile will against that person. To see a demonic force operating in a human life was not difficult in the ancient world. Many people considered the cosmos to be alive with spiritual beings, some benevolent and some malevolent. The good spirits could function as allies and guardians, the evil ones should be combatted as enemies bent on destruction. This life-and-death struggle with the demonic powers of the world is also assumed in the New Testament. One graphic description of the struggle against demons and spiritual powers is given in Ephesians 6:12: "For we are not contending against flesh and blood, but against the principalities, against the powers, against the world rulers of this present darkness, against the spiritual hosts of wickedness in the heavenly places." Hence, these wicked spirits active in human life must be fought, defeated, exorcised.

Exorcism was a common form of therapy in the ancient world. A person, or a spell, or an amulet of curative strength could be employed to counteract the ravages of an attacking demonic force. Essentially exorcism involves the use of power: the power of the exorcist is pitted against that of the demon—one authority, one will, one spirit against another. Exorcism is spiritual war, and as such it is not a pretty business, but involves potent language and strong adjurations. The exorcism, if successful, finally destroys the evil grip upon the patient's life, and restores such a person to wholeness once again.

One of the clearest examples I am familiar with of a spell for exorcism is the following ancient charm. It is written in Greek (and Coptic, or Egyptian: the prayer to God is given in the holy language of Egypt), and included along with dozens of other spells in a handbook, or "cookbook," from the working library of a magician and exorcist:

> Excellent charm for driving out demons.
> Formula to be spoken over the patient's head: Place olive branches before him, and stand behind him and say, "*Hail, God of Abraham; hail, God of Isaac; hail, God of Jacob; Jesus*

Christ, the Holy Spirit, the Son of the Father, who is above the Seven, who is within the Seven. Bring Yao Sabaoth; may your power issue forth from NN, *until you drive away this unclean demon Satan, who is in him.* I adjure you, demon, whoever you are, by this god, Sabarbarbathioth Sabarbarbathiouth Sabarbarbathioneth Sabarbarbaphai. Come out, demon, whoever you are, and stay away from NN—now, now! immediately, immediately! Come out, demon, since I bind you with unbreakable adamantine fetters, and I deliver you into the black chaos in perdition."

Procedure: Take seven olive branches. For six of them tie together the two ends of each one, but for the remaining one use it like a whip as you utter the adjuration. Keep it secret; it is proven.

After driving out the demon, hang around NN an amulet, which the patient puts on after the expulsion of the demon, with these things written on tin foil: "Bor Phor Phorba Phor Phorba Bes Charin Baubo Te Phor Borphorba Phorbabor Baphorba Phabraie Phorba Pharba Phorphor Phorba Bophor Phorba Phorphor Phorba Boborborba Pamphorba Phorphor Phorba, protect NN." There is also another amulet on which this sign occurs: ⛥

Most of the typical features of an exorcism are included within this ancient spell. The exorcist first invokes the power of God, and here makes use of the authoritative name of Jesus in attempting to overcome the demon (cf. Luke 10:17, where the seventy emissaries rejoice that the demons are undone by the name of Jesus; also Luke 9:49–50, where a person not of the circle of disciples is casting out demons in Jesus' name). Then the exorcist addresses the demon, "whoever you are"; the possession of the name of the demon would give the exorcist even more control over it. The terms used against the evil spirit are strong and demanding, with no polite social amenities: come out now! The demon is bound (cf. Mark 3:27 and parallels), and driven forth from the patient. And, lest the demon return once again to haunt the one formerly possessed, steps are taken to guarantee that the patient will never be bothered by the evil spirit again (cf. Luke 11:24–26; Matt. 12:43–45).

It is in this world of demons and exorcists that Jesus, too, performed his deeds of power.

* * *

According to the New Testament Gospels, Jesus was a faith-healer who healed the sick and cast out demons by means of the power of God. Not only did Jesus announce the kingdom of God and teach about the appropriate life in anticipation of the coming kingdom, but he also was a man of mighty deeds, and gained renown for helping those around him who were afflicted.

The account in Mark 5:1–20 of an exorcism in the area around Gerasa or Gadara (the manuscripts vary in naming the residents Gerasenes, Gadarenes, or Gergesenes) is a good representation of Jesus in action against the demons. A possessed man, violent and uncontrollable, engages in a battle of adjurations with Jesus. Jesus orders the demon, "Come out of the man, you unclean spirit" (5:8), and the victim in turn adjures Jesus to leave him alone (5:7). Jesus, however, assumes the upper hand in the violent struggle when he demands the name of the demon. Thus the exorcism is accomplished, and the patient is restored to health and sanity.

A nice touch is given to the story by the entry of the demonic forces into the herd of pigs (5:11–13). In a Jewish context there could be no more appropriate place for filthy spirits to live! Yet more may be said about this portion of the story. It is not unusual for exorcists to require a demon to provide some external proof that it actually has left the possessed person, and is not merely throwing its voice, like a deceptive and diabolical ventriloquist. One first-century miracle-worker, Apollonios of Tyana, exorcised a possessed lad whose demon induced raucous laughter and in-appropriate behavior, and demanded that the demon knock over a statue as proof of having truly exited from the boy. Another first-century exorcist, a Jewish fellow named Eleazar, had a demon overturn a basin of water as evidence of its departure.

Obviously Jesus achieved considerable notoriety as an effective worker of exorcisms and other wonders. Some people came to him for aid, some were skeptical about his abilities, and others believed in him in one way or another. Several interpretations of Jesus as exorcist appear on the pages of the Synoptic Gospels. Certain of his contemporaries apparently scoffed at Jesus as a crazy man who was out of his mind (Mark 3:20–21), while others accused him of harnessing the powers of the dead (Mark 6:14) or the devil (Mark 3:22). (The spirits of those who died untimely or violent deaths, it was thought, were restless and angry forces. Some people apparently proposed that Jesus had access to precisely such a spirit, namely that of the executed John the Baptist. Furthermore, plenty of magicians in the ancient world practiced black magic, or otherwise manipulated the infernal spirits for good or for ill. Thus the charge that Jesus exploited the power of "the prince of demons" is thoroughly comprehensible in a first-century context.) Still others may even have understood Jesus as the "son of David" in the light of his exorcisms and miracles (e.g., Mark 10:47–48). After all, Solomon son of David had outstanding fame among many Jewish people as a theurgist and conjurer, and not a few people were convinced that he had built the Jewish Temple by forcing the demons to work for him. Could Jesus, then, have been perceived by his acquaintances as a latter-day Solomon, and in that sense also a "son of David"?

What is clear is that the exorcistic ministry of Jesus is to be associated with his proclamation of a kingdom that is, in his words, "near." According to Luke 11:20, Jesus makes this connection explicit in a passage that sheds light upon the issue of the present and future dimensions to the kingdom: "if it is by the finger of God that I cast out demons, then the kingdom of God has come upon you." Here Jesus as exorcist claims most vividly (cf. Exod. 8:19) that the power of God comes to expression in the mighty deeds that Jesus is accomplishing, and that thereby the kingdom of God also reveals itself. In fact, Jesus says, the kingdom is becoming a reality now, as the reign of darkness is being overcome and the reign of God is being achieved. For where the enslaved are freed by Jesus from their servitude, there the kingdom of God is experienced.

*   *   *

If Jesus of Nazareth was an exorcist and wonder-worker, the New Testament evangelists rethink and reinterpret his role in several ways. We surely can understand the need for such reinterpretation when we observe that some early Christians were so dazzled by the majestic image of Jesus triumphant over the powers of evil that they became preoccupied with it. For such Christians Jesus was the winner par excellence, and they, too, hoped to be victorious in their own struggles with the hostile forces of the world by tapping into his power. Numerous magical amulets and papyri fashioned by these sorts of Christians have survived from the ancient period. Such Christian charms often include a prayer or invocation directed to Jesus, that the same potency which gave him mastery over the world might likewise bring success in the everyday lives of the Christians wearing the charms around their necks or carrying them on their persons.

In their enthusiasm for the triumphant Jesus, these "success-oriented" Christians collected edifying stories of Jesus' miracles and used them in a devotional and inspirational way. I would propose that two such collections may be detected when we examine the New Testament Gospels carefully. The first collection is reflected in the Gospel of John. Scholars often refer to these miracle stories as a Johannine "signs" collection, because the mighty deeds of Jesus are given the special term "signs" (John 2:11, 23; 4:54, etc.). Furthermore, the miraculous signs are numbered: the miracle at Cana is number one (2:11), the healing of the nobleman's son is number two (4:54), and presumably the further signs might also be assigned numbers. The point of this collection of miracle stories is emphasized in an oft-repeated statement in John: people believed when they saw the signs Jesus did (cf. 2:23; 6:14; 11:45–47). The same point is made in what may have been the conclusion to the signs collection, John 20:30–31. As this passage puts it, "Now Jesus did many other signs in the presence of his disciples, which are not written in this book; but these are written that you may believe that Jesus is the Christ, the Son of God. . . ."

Another collection of stories about Jesus' wonders seems to be discernible in the Gospel of Mark. As we analyze chapters 5 and 7, we notice that a series of miracle stories is presented, often with one account coming on the heels of another. This mini-catalog of miracle stories suggests that Mark, too, knew of a collection of anecdotes presenting Jesus as healer and exorcist.

John and Mark, and through Mark, Matthew and Luke, thus had at their disposal anthologies of miracle stories; but they did not simply adopt the wonder-working perspective of these collections. Rather, they each edited and revised the literary materials they were using as they composed their Gospels, shaping the materials to accord with their own special interpretation of the significance of Jesus.

We turn briefly to these interpretations of John, Mark, and Matthew. (I omit Luke from the present discussion. Let me only say that he rather appreciates the world view of magic, miracle, and exorcism, and underscores the need for Christians to avail themselves of the superior power and authority of Jesus; cf. the potent abilities of the apostles and Paul in Acts.)

For John the dictum of the signs collection, "seeing is believing," was not an acceptable understanding of Christian faith. John even singles out Thomas, who has been nicknamed "doubting Thomas" ever since, to emphasize that there is much more to faith than the belief occasioned by a marvel that may be observed. Jesus announces, "Blessed are those who have not seen and yet believe" (20:29). John portrays Jesus shying away from those who believe just because of signs: "Jesus did not trust himself to them, because he knew all people and needed no one to bear witness of people; for he himself knew what was in people" (2:24–25). Instead, the Johannine narrative continues, Jesus was much more concerned about spiritual realities. In the story of Nicodemus (unique to John's Gospel) this character applauds Jesus because of his signs (3:2), but is made to turn his attention away from the more mundane matters, the "earthly things" like showy signs, to the more exalted matters, the "heavenly things" like eternal life. And as Nicodemus considers a new interpretation of the meaning of Christ, so also John hopes that his readers will believe that Jesus is not just a flashy performer of signs, but rather the very Word of God.

As we have already remarked, Jesus in the Gospel of John speaks in "I am" discourses. In the present discussion it is interesting to note that the self-predications of Jesus may also assist in the spiritual reinterpretation of the signs. Thus Jesus does a sign with wine (2:1–11), but he also declares, "I am the true vine" (15:1). Jesus feeds a multitude (6:1–14), but he also claims, "I am the bread of life" (6:35). Jesus gives sight to a blind man (9:1–12), but he also says, "I am the light of the world" (8:12). And Jesus raises the dead (11:1–45), but he also proclaims, "I am the resurrection and the life" (11:25). In other words, John uses the discourses of Jesus to turn the attention of his readers even further away from the worldly wonders, so that the readers might meet the transcendent wonder-worker who is so exalted that he is in the Father (10:38; 17:21) and is one with the Father (10:30).

Mark, too, modifies the perspective of the miracle-story collection included in his Gospel. For Mark it is not enough to confess that Jesus is a son of God in the sense of a successful miracle-worker. Plenty of people in the ancient world flaunted such pedigrees, and made claims of being "divine men." Alexander the Great allegedly was the son of Zeus, Plato was the son of Apollo, and some said Apollonios of Tyana also was the offspring of the great god Zeus. No, according to Mark the paradox of the gospel is that the miracle-working Son of God, Jesus, is precisely the one who suffered and died upon the cross. Mark is too committed to a theology of the cross to adopt without qualification a theology of power and success like that of his anthology of miracle stories.

Mark's well-known theme of the "Messianic secret" aids in the communication of his Christology. Repeatedly in the Gospel of Mark Jesus warns witnesses to the miracles (5:43; 7:36), his disciples (8:30), and even demons (3:12) not to proclaim who he is. They are to keep secret that he is Christ, or the Son of God. Initially this seems odd. It seems even more so when we reflect upon the purpose of miracle stories: the confession and praise at the conclusion of a typical miracle story are meant to exalt the figure of the miracle-worker, and this confessional climax is stripped away in Mark's Gospel. The real punch is missing from many of Mark's accounts of Jesus' wondrous deeds, and the anticipated applause is muffled by the command of silence.

The narrative of events taking place near Caesarea Philippi (8:27–33) constitutes a major turning point in the plot of the Gospel. Following one such exhortation to silence (8:30), Jesus provides the first prediction of his passion, and he introduces another title well known from such apocalyptic books as Daniel (e.g., 7:13): the Son of Man. Mark stresses that now, in speaking of the cross, Jesus did not resort to secrecy or silence, but "he said this plainly." When Peter, or for that matter any believer who might be scandalized by a theology of the cross, begs to disagree with Jesus' talk of his suffering, he is sternly rebuked for his improper understanding of the true role of Jesus (8:33).

We may be able to comprehend, then, what Mark seeks to accomplish in his Gospel. He preaches Christ the Son of God, but he literally silences the enthusiasm that might be prompted by such a claim with his insistence that this Jesus is also the suffering Son of Man.

Near the conclusion of his Gospel, Mark interjects a small but decisive scene within the crucifixion account. In 15:39 he states that the centurion who was witnessing the suffering and death of Jesus commented publicly, "Truly this man was the Son of God!" Here at last is a clear resolution of what Mark means to proclaim from the very beginning of his "gospel of Jesus Christ, the Son of God" (1:1). The secret finally is out. The true confession of Jesus, given by a centurion, a Gentile, professes that Jesus is to be seen as Son of God *at the cross*, that is, specifically within the context of his passion. For Mark, the proper Christology must embrace not only the miracle-worker but also the crucified one of Golgotha.

Finally, Matthew is also somewhat suspicious of a wonder-working emphasis, particularly when the distasteful details of miracle stories might suggest that a crude sort of magic is being advocated. As a result, Matthew tends to edit out of his account those descriptive items which could lead a reader to think that Jesus was nothing but a common magician or sorcerer. Since Matthew was especially chary of exorcisms, we might take a look once again at the accounts of the exorcism near Gerasa (or Gadara), in order to see how Matthew (8:28–34) reworks Mark's account (5:1–20).

In general, Matthew removes many of the key features of this vivid story as preserved in Mark. The unpleasant description of the life of the demon-possessed man is omitted (cf. Mark 5:3–5; Luke 8:29). Actually, Matthew posits that *two* men are possessed (8:28) rather than one as in Mark and Luke, thus solving the problem of the plurality of the demons ("Legion," Mark 5:9 and Luke 8:30) by distributing a demon each to more than one person instead of having more than one demon gang up on a single victim. The battle of adjurations between Jesus and the demon-possessed, as described in Mark 5:7–8, is revised in Matthew 8:29 into a fairly polite question addressed to Jesus. Even the crucial words of exorcism, and the possession of the demonic name (cf. Mark 5:8–9), are absent from Matthew's abbreviated, domesticated account. As we may easily conclude, what is an instance of exorcistic struggle in Mark has become a simple matter of demonic flight in Matthew. If I may overstate the case just a bit, Matthew's demons obtain the permission of Jesus, and emigrate into the pigs and their own eventual destruction.

*　　*　　*

To return to the title of this chapter: on the basis of the New Testament evidence we may conclude that the historical Jesus of Nazareth was indeed an exorcist. The authors of the Gospels, however, fashioned their interpretations of their wonder-working Savior by reshaping the accounts of miracles and exorcisms. Thus they proclaimed their own understanding of the mighty Jesus who was the object of their faith and worship.

A good though deliberately controversial account of magical traditions and miraculous events in the ancient world of Jesus may be found in Morton Smith, *Jesus the Magician* (San Francisco: Harper & Row, 1978). The worthy book by John M. Hull, *Hellenistic Magic and the Synoptic Tradition* (Naperville: Allenson, 1974), is less flamboyant but more exegetically sound. The translation of the spell for exorcism is my own, and will appear in a collection of such texts edited by Hans Dieter Betz. The life of the exorcist Apollonios of Tyana, written by Philostratus, is readily available in Cartlidge and Dungan, *Documents for the Study of the Gospels* (Philadelphia: Fortress, 1980), pp. 205–42.

Robert T. Fortna, *The Gospel of Signs* (London: Cambridge Univ. Press, 1970), has discussed in detail the collection of miracle stories used in the composition of the Gospel of John.

5

HOW MANY DONKEYS
DID JESUS RIDE?

*The triumphal entry and the fulfillment
of prophecy*

ALL four of the New Testament Gospels introduce their accounts
of the last days of Jesus with the exciting story of the triumphal
entry into Jerusalem. We celebrate this event each liturgical year
on a day designated as Palm Sunday, but were it not for the Gospel
of John, we would have neither the palms nor the Sunday! For
while the Synoptic Gospels of Mark and Matthew merely mention
unspecified leaves or branches (Mark 11:8; Matt. 21:8) gathered
on an unspecified day, John refers both to palms (12:13) and to
Sunday (12:12, "the next day," in the context of 12:1, "six days
before the Passover").

The story of the triumphal entry is fundamentally the story of
a nationalistic demonstration, with Jesus playing a key role. At the
time of the Feast of the Passover, often an occasion for patriotic
fervor and even messianic hope for the Jewish people, the usual
pilgrims were on their way to the holy city of Jerusalem to celebrate. We can imagine the intensity of feeling when we recall
that these pilgrims, restive under the foreign occupation of the
Romans, were celebrating the Exodus, the liberation of the Hebrew people from captivity in Egypt. Under such circumstances
the emotions can surge and the pulse can quicken.

One of these pilgrims was the teacher and exorcist from Galilee, Jesus of Nazareth, approaching Jerusalem with his band of
followers. Devoted in word and deed to the coming of the kingdom of God, Jesus and his fellow travelers must have felt an
incredible thrill as they entered the city that was the symbol of
all their desires and expectations. Shouts of joy rang out, and
acclamations of "Hosanna" filled the air as Jesus and his entourage
extolled the dawning of the kingdom. In the cries of "Hosanna!
Blessed is he who comes in the name of the Lord!" (Mark 11:9),
the celebrants not only were entering into the spirit of the oc-

casion but they were also uttering an exclamation (Ps. 118:25–26) that typically resounded during holidays like Passover. One thing led to another, and all four New Testament accounts, from their differing perspectives, agree that Jesus himself came riding on donkey-back, as a harbinger of God's reign. As the evangelists describe it, the King is coming with the kingdom!

The four accounts of the triumphal entry agree substantially about the nature and significance of this event. Yet from their various emphases and interpretations much can be learned about what they each wish to accentuate in their proclamations of Jesus. Hence we shall examine, with some exactness, certain features of these four parallel passages: Mark 11:1–10, Matthew 21:1–9, Luke 19:28–40, and John 12:12–19.

As we study these passages, we observe at once that the most substantial agreements exist among the Synoptics, and that John, as usual, diverges from the other Gospels. In the opening verses of Mark, Matthew, and Luke only rather minor variations are to be noted: slight differences in wording (more obvious in the Greek than in the English), Matthew's omission of Bethany, and so on. (Matthew's two donkeys within these verses will occupy our attention presently.) One minute but interesting matter relates to the end of the directions given by Jesus in Mark 11:3 and Matthew 21:3. Matthew modifies Mark very slightly, but he probably understands the conclusion of the statement ("and he will send them immediately") as describing the response of the donkey-owner rather than the action of Jesus (as in Mark). Matthew continues (21:5), unlike the other Synoptic Gospels but more like John (12:15), with a citation of prophecy, introduced with Matthew's usual formula for fulfillment of prophecy ("This took place to fulfill what was spoken by the prophet ...").

After this Matthean insertion, the Synoptic parallels resume as before. The preparations are described (in a shortened form in Matthew), and the triumphal entry is about to begin. The size of the group accompanying Jesus is not made clear in Mark ("many ... others ..."), but Matthew and Luke use words like "crowds" and "multitude" to highlight the massive proportions of the gathering. Similarly, Mark has the people give praise with Hosannas, and focuses upon the coming kingdom (11:9–10). The blessing upon him "who comes in the name of the Lord" (cf. Ps. 118:26) is spoken of Jesus, and though it remains somewhat ambiguous, it implies that the kingdom is coming to expression in the figure

MARK 11:1-10

And when they drew near to Jerusalem, to Bethphage and Bethany, at the Mount of Olives, he sent two of his disciples, and said to them, "Go into the village opposite you, and immediately as you enter it you will find a colt tied, on which no one has ever sat; untie it and bring it. If any one says to you, 'Why are you doing this?' say, 'The Lord has need of it and will send it back here immediately.'"

MATTHEW 21:1-9

And when they drew near to Jerusalem and came to Bethphage, to the Mount of Olives, then Jesus sent two disciples, saying to them, "Go into the village opposite you, and immediately you will find an ass tied, and a colt with her; untie them and bring them to me. If any one says anything to you, you shall say, 'The Lord has need of them,' and he will send them immediately."

This took place to fulfill what was spoken by the prophet, saying, "Tell the daughter of Zion, Behold, your king is coming to you, humble, and mounted on an ass, and on a colt, the foal of an ass." The disciples went and did as Jesus had directed them;

LUKE 19:28-40

And when he had said this, he went on ahead, going up to Jerusalem. When he drew near to Bethphage and Bethany, at the mount that is called Olivet, he sent two of the disciples, saying, "Go into the village opposite, where on entering you will find a colt tied, on which no one has ever yet sat; untie it and bring it here. If any one asks you, 'Why are you untying it?' you shall say this, 'The Lord has need of it.'"

JOHN 12:12-19

The next day a great crowd who had come to the feast heard that Jesus was coming to Jerusalem.

cf. 12:15

45

they brought the ass and the colt, and put their garments on them, and he sat on them. Most of the crowd spread their garments on the road, and others cut branches from the trees and spread them on the road.

And the crowds that went before him and that followed him shouted, "Hosanna to the Son of David! Blessed is he who comes in the name of the Lord! Hosanna in the highest!"

And they went away, and found a colt tied at the door out in the open street; and those who stood there said to them, "What are you doing, untying the colt?" And they told them what Jesus had said; and they let them go. And they brought the colt to Jesus, and threw their garments on it; and he sat upon it. And many spread their garments on the road, and others spread leafy branches which they had cut from the fields.

And those who went before and those who followed cried out, "Hosanna! Blessed is he who comes in the name of the Lord! Blessed is the kingdom of our father David that is coming! Hosanna in the highest!"

So those who were sent went away and found it as he had told them. And as they were untying the colt, its owners said to them, "Why are you untying the colt?" And they said, "The Lord has need of it." And they brought it to Jesus, and throwing their garments on the colt they set Jesus upon it. And as he rode along, they spread their garments on the road.

As he was now drawing near, at the descent of the Mount of Olives, the whole multitude of the disciples began to rejoice and praise God with a loud voice for all the mighty works that they had seen, saying, "Blessed is the King who comes in the name of the Lord! Peace in heaven and glory in the highest!"

So they took branches of palm trees and went out to meet him, crying, "Hosanna! Blessed is he who comes in the name of the Lord, even the King of Israel!"

cf. 11:7

cf. 21:7

cf. 21:5

cf. 19:35

And Jesus found a young ass and sat upon it; as it is written, "Fear not, daughter of Zion; behold, your king is coming, sitting on an ass's colt!" His disciples did not understand this at first; but when Jesus was glorified, then they remembered that this had been written of him and had been done to him. The crowd that had been with him when he called Lazarus out of the tomb and raised him from the dead bore witness. The reason why the crowd went to meet him was that they heard he had done this sign. The Pharisees then said to one another, "You see that you can do nothing; look, the world has gone after him."

cf. 21:14–16

And some of the Pharisees in the multitude said to him, "Teacher, rebuke your disciples." He answered, "I tell you, if these were silent, the very stones would cry out."

47

of Jesus. Matthew and Luke remove any ambiguity by specifying that this nationalistic parade is a specifically messianic demonstration. Matthew turns the attention away from the kingdom of David (Mark 11:10) and instead directs the Hosanna to "the Son of David" (Matt. 21:9). Whatever "Son of David" could possibly mean in other, exorcistic settings, here this famous title of Jesus is used in the more usual, messianic sense: Jesus is the King, the royal Messiah of the house of David! Jesus as Son of David is very important in Matthew's Gospel. From the opening verse of the Gospel, and the subsequent genealogy and birth account (cf. 1:20), Matthew shows that he prefers this messianic designation as a way to place Jesus squarely within the mainstream of Judaism. Luke, conversely, omits the Hosanna, and substitutes for it the Greek word for "glory" (19:38), which would naturally be more comprehensible to a Greek audience. Along with Matthew, Luke also puts the accent upon the King rather than the kingdom, and leaves no room for uncertainty in his revision of Mark (and thereby also Ps. 118:26): "Blessed is *the King* who comes in the name of the Lord!" (Luke 19:38).

John's version of the triumphal entry, unlike the Synoptic accounts, begins with the Hosannas and ends with the donkey. Like Matthew and Luke, John pictures "a great crowd" assembled (12:12), bearing their palm branches and shouting their Hosannas. (Within Judaism palm branches connoted patriotism; cf. 1 Macc. 13:51 and 2 Macc. 10:7, where we may read accounts of the celebrations of palm-carrying Jewish patriots during the Maccabean period.) Also like Luke, John stresses that "he who comes in the name of the Lord," that is, Jesus, is none other than "the King of Israel!" (12:13). After such exclamations Jesus mounts a donkey, in overt fulfillment of prophecy, says John 12:15 (cf. Zeph. 3:16–17 and Zech. 9:9), just as Matthew also insists. John then proceeds to make an extraordinary claim (12:16) about the meaning of this triumphal entry. At the time, he says, the significance of all these events was unclear. Only after the crucifixion and resurrection did the disciples realize the true import of Palm Sunday. John closes his account in his own way, with two profiles of the surrounding people: "the crowd" lingers around Jesus because of his signs, and the Pharisees admit that "the world" (a bit of hyperbole, but a fitting term for John; see 3:16–17) is following after Jesus.

These four New Testament passages thus represent two fairly

similar streams of tradition about the triumphal entry of Jesus: the Markan and the Johannine. Within the Markan tradition Matthew and Luke each edit Mark in order to make points they judge to be of some significance for syntax, clarity, or theology. John, on the other hand, complements the accounts of the Synoptics with his own perspectives and emphases.

*   *   *

The "Palmesel" of the triumphal entry is a small but familiar detail in the story. So popular is this beastly character that resourceful entrepreneurs in Palestine still provide "sacred" donkeys for tourists to hire in the vicinity of the Mount of Olives. Within the story the donkey on which Jesus rides is part of the accumulation of features giving a royal cast to the account. As the spreading of garments is an honor sometimes bestowed on kings (rather like a clothier's red carpet; cf. 2 Kings 9:13), and Hosannas can be addressed to royalty (cf. 2 Sam. 14:4; 2 Kings 6:26), so also the image of Jesus entering Jerusalem on a donkey recalls the kingly prophecies of Zechariah 9:9:

> Rejoice greatly, O daughter of Zion!
> Shout aloud, O daughter of Jerusalem!
> Lo, your king comes to you,
> triumphant and victorious is he,
> humble and riding on an ass,
> on a colt the foal of an ass.

Explicitly (Matthew and John) or implicitly (Mark and Luke), all four New Testament evangelists show themselves to be informed by the promises and implications of this Old Testament prophet.

If Jesus thus is seated on donkey-back, the question then emerges: how many donkeys did Jesus ride? For while Mark, Luke, and John concur that Jesus rode on one donkey, Matthew consistently mentions two donkeys. Actually, a few late manuscripts recognize the problem of too many donkeys in Matthew, and change the text so that it is in harmony with the other Gospels. But these harmonizing manuscripts provide neither early nor secure readings. Similarly, the Revised Standard Version of Matthew 21:7, which I modified slightly above, obscures the problem with the translation "and he sat thereon."

The answer to our question about the number of donkeys may

be found when we examine Matthew's concern for the fulfillment of Scripture. More than any other of the evangelists Matthew
wishes to relate the life and teachings of Jesus to the promises of
the Old Testament prophets, and more often than not he does so
explicitly with a quotation formula such as we have already no-
ticed in 21:5. Thus it is almost predictable that Matthew would
cite Zechariah 9:9 (with Isa. 62:11: "Say to the daughter of Zion
...") as documentation for his understanding of Jesus as the King
promised by the Hebrew prophets.

Zechariah 9:9 is Hebrew poetry, and as such it illustrates typical
literary conventions, most notably poetic parallelism. Hebrew poetry seeks to express the same or similar ideas in lines that are
balanced and parallel with each other. The full idea is not expressed in any single line, but rather in the several lines that are
combined to form a poetic unit. Consider, for instance,
Psalm 19:1–2:

> The heavens are telling the glory of God,
> and the firmament proclaims his handiwork.
> Day to day pours forth speech,
> and night to night declares knowledge.

These four poetic lines constitute two couplets. The first two and
the last two lines belong together, and each couplet expresses a
single essential idea (all the sky bears witness to the creator God;
day and night the world proclaims the knowledge of God). Again,
in Psalm 20:1,

> The Lord answer you in the day of trouble!
> The name of the God of Jacob protect you,

the message of the couplet is: may God save you!

In just this fashion Zechariah 9:9 speaks poetically of the coming of a king. Three couplets communicate three thoughts: (1) be
glad, (2) for your victorious king is coming (3) on a simple donkey. Zechariah writes of only one donkey, but does so in two
parallel poetic lines. The Gospel of John understands Zechariah
correctly: John refers to one donkey only, and in his paraphrase
of Zechariah he cites only one of the poetic lines, and so has just
the "ass's colt" (12:15) to worry about.

Matthew, on the other hand, quotes Zechariah 9:9 with considerable accuracy. Either Matthew did not understand Hebrew
poetic conventions sufficiently, or else he wished to be faithful to

the very letter of the prophetic text. Whatever is the case, Matthew counted the number of donkeys in Zechariah, and wrote his account on the basis of this numeration. Because of his understanding of Zechariah, he revised Mark's account to allow for a literal correlation with prophecy. Not that Matthew is concerned much about donkeys per se. He certainly does not wish to visualize Jesus on two donkeys, as a first-century circus performer. Rather, Matthew uses his two donkeys to communicate that Jesus' triumphal entry happened entirely within the plan and purpose of God.

Obviously, the implications of this analysis of Matthew for the role of prophecy and fulfillment in the early church are tremendous. What I am suggesting is that in order to understand prophecy and its fulfillment we need to consider not only the prescience of the prophet as it comes to a realization in the life of Jesus or the church, but also the faith of the evangelist who looks for guidance from the prophets in writing his Gospel. The New Testament authors who assert that events "took place to fulfill what was spoken by the prophets" are saying as much about their own faith as the predictive powers of the prophets. These writers are claiming that they understand themselves and the church in the light of the promises of God in history, and that they shape and reshape their literary works according to these divine promises. For Matthew and the other New Testament authors do not simply record history; they interpret and compose it from the vantage point of God's promises and God's salvation.

For the sake of such a comparative study of the four Gospels as we have undertaken in this chapter, a good synopsis of the Gospels in parallel columns, like that of Burton H. Throckmorton, *Gospel Parallels* (Nashville: Nelson, 1979), is indispensable. Even more helpful is one with the Greek, such as Kurt Aland, *Synopsis Quattuor Evangeliorum* (New York: United Bible Societies, 1978); or, with the Greek and English, Kurt Aland, *Synopsis of the Four Gospels: Greek-English Edition of the Synopsis Quattuor Evangeliorum with the Text of the Revised Standard Version* (New York: United Bible Societies, 1979).

Several good commentaries exist for each of the four Gospels, and these should supplement the study of the texts. I might suggest a few fine series: The International Critical Commentary is an old standard among commentaries, the Pelican Gospel Commentaries and the Proclamation Commentaries are helpful (and in inexpensive paperback editions), and the New International Commentary includes some fine volumes written by evangelical scholars. Besides these works I should highlight a handful of other helpful commentaries: Eduard Schweizer, *The Good News according to Matthew* (Atlanta: John Knox, 1975); C. E. B. Cranfield, *The Gospel according to Saint Mark* (Cambridge: Cambridge Univ. Press, 1972); Vincent Taylor, *The Gospel according to St. Mark* (New York: St. Martin's, 1966); Joseph A. Fitzmyer, *The Gospel according to Luke* (Garden City: Doubleday, 1981), the first of two Anchor Bible volumes; and Raymond E. Brown, *The Gospel according to John* (Garden City: Doubleday, 1966, 1970), an exemplary commentary also in two volumes of the Anchor Bible series. For other suggestions see Scholer, *A Basic Bibliographic Guide for New Testament Exegesis* (Grand Rapids: Eerdmans, 1973), pp. 74–77. We await, with considerable anticipation, the appearance of commentaries on the Gospels in the excellent Hermeneia series being published by Fortress Press.

6

WHEN WILL
THIS WORLD END?

Jesus and early Christian apocalyptic

THE centuries just before, during, and after Jesus lived were trying times for many Jewish people. The period of the Babylonian exile, when the unthinkable not only was thought but also was experienced by the people of "the promised land," prompted the Hebrew poets to utter bitter laments over the fate of the people of Yahweh. Psalm 137 is one of the most melancholy of these expressions of sorrow and rage:

> By the waters of Babylon,
> there we sat down and wept,
> when we remembered Zion.
> On the willows there
> we hung up our lyres.

Even the hate-filled "beatitudes" at the end of the lament (hardly edifying material for a sermon or meditation) are understandable as cries of revenge over the loss of the holy city, holy land, and holy lives:

> O daughter of Babylon, you devastator!
> Happy shall he be who requites you
> with what you have done to us!
> Happy shall he be who takes your little ones
> and dashes them against the rock!

During the latter part of the sixth century B.C.E., however, some of these exiles returned from their captivity (and some did not: hence the Babylonian school of Judaism and the Babylonian Talmud). But they arrived back in Palestine only to face more opposition, as local forces and armies from abroad vied for control of this vital region in the Middle East.

To this day the devastation of Palestine and the battle for Jerusalem remain the grimmest of realities in Middle Eastern life. As I write these words, hostile forces are arrayed against Beirut,

Lebanon, and the age-old agony in the Middle East continues. One moving commemoration of the devastation of Jerusalem has been presented recently as a "son et lumière" performance in the old city. Entitled "A Stone in David's Tower," this dramatic reading with sound and light enumerates the empires and conquerors who have ravaged the city. As the sounds of war echo in the background, voices recite the brutal role:

The hosts of Pharaoh from the South
The chariots of Assyria from the North
The armies of Babylon
The armies of Persia
The Macedonians
The Hellenic Kingdom of the Seleucids, from the North
The Hellenic Kingdom of the Ptolemies, from the South
The Roman Empire, master of the world
The Byzantine Empire, defender of Christianity and protector of the Holy Sepulchre
The Persian Lord of War
The Great Caliph, Omar Ibn Khatab, out of the Arabian desert with the sword and the new message of Islam
The Caliphs of the House of Omayyad, of the House of Abbas, of the House of Fatima
The Sultans of Egypt
The Seljuk Turks
The Crusaders — Knights of Lorraine, Flanders, Provence, Normandy, Sicily
The Knights Templars, the Hospitallers
The Saracens
The Franks
The Mongol hordes out of Asia
The Mameluke Emirs
The Sultan Salim the First, ruler of Constantinople
The Ottoman Empire, master of all the lands from the Danube to the Nile
The British Empire, on which the sun never sets
The Arab Legion of the Hashemite Kingdom of Jordan.

To be sure, the pro-Israeli bias is obvious, especially near the conclusion of the list. Still, the litany expresses with painful clarity the suffering and oppression that have been borne by the people of Palestine since ancient times.

Perhaps darkest of ancient times for the Jewish people were the days of the Seleucid King Antiochus IV (175–164 B.C.E.), called

54

"Epiphanes" because he thought of himself as the epiphany, or the manifestation, of god. Antiochus, a devotee of Greek culture and an advocate of the Hellenizing process, employed ruthless tactics when necessary to encourage his subjects to embrace the styles and values of Greek life. Ever since Alexander the Great of Macedon had inaugurated a brave new world by opening channels of communication and influence between the Greek and the Middle Eastern spheres, many residents of this "ecumenical" world (a term used in the ancient world of Alexander, too) hurried to take upon themselves the trappings of polite, "civilized" society—Greek trappings. Such people donned appropriate Greek attire, and learned (more or less) to speak the Greek language in place of their own "barbarian" tongue. (The term "barbarian" is also a Greek term, and was applied to all people who were not Greek, that is, whose language sounded to Greek ears like "bar-bar.") But dress and language, as we know, are only the outward expressions of a whole complex of social and cultural values. So these Greek-speaking "barbarians" who wore togas often adopted cultural and religious habits that coincided with their newly found cosmopolitanism. They exercised and dialogued at the gymnasium, cheered at the games, applauded the famous playwrights at the theater, and worshiped the Greek gods at the temple.

Some Jewish people, wishing also to be good Hellenists, joined up with this movement. They faced all the same difficulties encountered by others in the Middle East who wanted to live like the Greeks, and more so. To give one example of the unique problems faced by a Jewish Hellenist: a Jewish athlete who wished to participate in the international games would naturally be expected to run in the nude just like everyone else. Yet the circumcised Jew would be quite obvious among so many uncircumcised Greeks. Consequently, Jewish doctors developed techniques in plastic surgery allowing them to disguise a circumcision, so that a Jewish male could race incognito.

To other Jewish people, who saw in the Hellenization movement a betrayal of Jewish religion and life-style, such shame and disrespect for the visible sign of God's covenant, circumcision, was intolerable. One person who felt this way was the author of 1 Maccabees. In describing the Jewish Hellenists, he writes, "In those days lawless people came forth from Israel, and misled many" (1:11). According to 1 Maccabees, these Jewish people were unfaithful to the Torah, renegades who capitulated to the customs of the Gentiles, "and removed the marks of circumcision, and abandoned the holy covenant. They joined with the Gentiles and sold themselves to do evil" (1:15). The struggle over Hellenization had become a problem of Jew opposed to fellow Jew.

Antiochus Epiphanes was totally in support of the Hellenistic Jewish movement, and determined to consolidate his power along the lines of enforcing Hellenization upon all the Jewish people. When his initial efforts in this direction proved insufficient, he decided in 167 B.C.E. to break the resistance of the stubborn "parochial" Jews who refused to Hellenize. He ordered "that all should be one people, and that each should give up his or her customs" (1 Macc. 1:41–42), and backed up his order with stern and cruel measures. The essential features of Judaism were declared illegal: sacrifices, Sabbath observance, religious holidays, and circumcision were forbidden, upon pain of death. Furthermore, copies of the Torah were torn and burned, those observant of Torah were executed, and Jewish people were made to eat pork and worship at unholy shrines. But his ultimate sacrilege was the erection of an altar to Zeus upon the sacred altar of burnt offering in the second Jewish Temple in Jerusalem—"a desolating sacrilege," as 1 Maccabees 1:54 describes it.

The Jewish people, even the little children, suffered and died horribly. 1 Maccabees summarizes the grievous situation in Palestine and the determination of the people in a terse but moving paragraph:

> Many in Israel stood firm and were resolved in their hearts not to eat unclean food. They chose to die rather than to be defiled by food or to profane the holy covenant; and they did die. And very great wrath came upon Israel. (1:62–64)

Great wrath can spawn a great response, and so it was among the Jewish people. One response was the mighty revolt of those called the Maccabees, namely, Mattathias, his sons (one was named Judas Maccabeus, "the hammerer," whence the term "Maccabees"), and their warriors. The climax of the revolt occurred in the month Chislev of 164 B.C.E.: the profaned Temple was cleansed, restored, and dedicated once again to the proper worship of Yahweh (1 Macc. 4:52–58). To this day the festival of Hanukkah celebrates the rededication of the Temple.

Another response to the wrath was what I have already alluded to in a previous chapter as the apocalyptic movement. Some Jewish thinkers wished to proclaim hope; but seeing no real possiblity for hope within this world, they looked for God to intervene in order to bring the divine plan to its completion in the kingdom of God. The kings of this world cause only grief, it was thought. The King of all, however, will bring a new world that will overturn the inequities and injustices experienced now, and usher in a wondrous new age of glory and righteousness. In the hell of human history, Jewish apocalyptic preachers spoke a word of reassurance to those in despair. Be of good cheer: the End is near, and God is coming soon!

The book of Daniel, and especially Daniel's visions, provide excellent examples of the characteristics of apocalyptic literature. It is widely held that the author of the book was living during the time of Antiochus Epiphanes and the Maccabean revolt, and that he was writing to inspire his Jewish readers with confidence and fortitude during those desperate years. Making use of the extensive symbolism typical of this sort of literature (so also in the New Testament apocalypse, the book of Revelation), the author of Daniel includes at the end of the book several visions that interpret recent history and announce future developments.

Consider, if you will, Daniel 7. Daniel's vision opens with a scene of cosmic upheaval—a destructive scene that is really a parody of Genesis 1, with its wind of God blowing over the surface of the water. Here in Daniel all four winds are howling, and the great primal sea of chaos is agitated (7:2). Out of this uneasy, aquatic abyss emerge four monstrous beasts: a winged lion, a bear, a winged leopard, and something like a dragon. Clearly these are symbolic beasts. The first represents the kingdom of the Babylonians, the second of the Medes, the third of the Persians, and the fourth of the Greeks—four kingdoms that were advocates of evil chaos, says the author, against the people of Israel. The arrival of the Greek dragon is the arrival of Alexander the Great (cf. the he-goat from the West in Dan. 8:5–8), and the dragon's ten horns symbolize ten successors of Alexander in the Seleucid Kingdom of the Middle East. A little horn sprouts up (7:8), which is none other than Antiochus IV himself, mocked as a runt among larger horns. Nonetheless, this little runt Antiochus was able to secure his rule by means of success in battle (v. 8: "three of the first horns were plucked up by the roots"), and he certainly did have "a mouth speaking great things" (namely, that he was Epiphanes). In addition, it is also mentioned in Daniel that this same Antiochus was the one who tried to "wear out the saints of the Most High" (7:25) by means of the atrocities he committed for three and a half years ("a time, two times, and half a time"), and who even set up "the abomination that makes desolate" in the holy Temple (9:27; 11:31; 12:11). At this point (7:9–10) the scene quickly shifts to God the glorious judge in heaven. He is, after all, still in charge of all that happens, even among the beasts of human history. Then immediately the scene changes once again. The beast on earth, the empire of Antiochus and the Hellenists, is destroyed, and the lives of the other beasts linger on for just a little longer.

The message of Daniel 7 is that at this very time, with the passing of Antiochus and the Seleucids and the final gasps of the other kingdoms of the earth, this world will come to an end! The reign of the beasts out of the sea has concluded, and now the vision points to the reign of the Man ("one like a son of man," 7:13) from heaven. From now on all action begins from above, and God and the Son of Man will act decisively. The kingdom of God is about to be inaugurated, and unlike the kingdoms of the earth, God's rule will be indestructible and everlasting (7:14, 27).

To paraphrase this vision of Daniel: the kingdom of God is near!

*　　*　　*

Jesus' proclamation of the kingdom finds its place within the context of apocalyptic. As we have been observing in these chapters, the announcement of a kingdom that is near at hand is front and center in the words and deeds of Jesus.

Yet Jesus also gives a special cast to his talk of the kingdom with his marvelous juxtaposition of present realities and future hopes. According to Jesus, the preaching of God's reign entails not only the wonderful expectation of future bliss; in some sense it also involves the present experience of a kingdom realized. The powers of evil are defeated, the sick are healed, and the sinners are forgiven: in these ways the power of the kingdom already is exhibiting itself. Matthew 11 and Luke 7 describe such manifestations of God's power with words taken over from Q (cf. also the promises about "that Day" of the Lord in Isa. 29:18–19; 35:5–6; 61:1). When John the Baptist inquires from prison, through his disciples, about whether Jesus is "he who is to come" (Matt. 11:3; Luke 7:19), that is, the Messiah, Jesus replies, "Go and tell John what you hear and see: the blind receive their sight and the lame walk, lepers are cleansed and the deaf hear, and the dead are raised up, and the poor have good news preached to them" (Matt. 11:4–5; cf. Luke 7:22).

The present realization of the kingdom of God is also declared in a singular passage in the Gospel of Luke: 17:20–21. This account reads as follows: "Being asked by the Pharisees when the kingdom of God was coming, he answered them, 'The kingdom of God is not coming with signs to be observed; nor will they say, "Lo, here it is!" or "There!" for behold, the kingdom of God is in the midst of you.' " The scene here presented presumably was as common among ancient apocalypticists as it still is among modern-day prophets of the end-time. The question or challenge is raised: When will the End come? This question has tantalized people for a long, long time, and to this day it is a query being addressed in sermons, radio and television programs, and magazines and books of all kinds. One of the most memorable and humorous presentations of this question must be that of Peter De Vries in *Let Me Count the Ways,* where Stan the skeptic is convinced by his fundamentalist wife that the world now is coming to an end, and repents fervently—only to discover later that the supposedly apocalyptic conflagration was nothing but a fire in the local fireworks factory. Stan then utters his most quotable line: "What you saw was not a sinner reviving but an atheist backsliding."

Jesus' answer to the Pharisees' question is both restrained and wise. To begin with, Jesus refuses (unlike so many latter-day apocalypticists since him) to speculate about the precise date when the kingdom will come. Nor does he encourage his questioners to read the "signs of the times" in order to compute the exact scenario leading to the end of the world. (As we shall see shortly, the same caution against undue speculation is recommended in the Synoptic apocalypse; cf. Mark 13:32–37 and parallels.) In fact, Jesus concludes, this kingdom of God is already present "in the midst of you."

Unfortunately, the meaning of the phrase "in the midst of you" is not entirely clear. Two translations would be quite possible from the Greek: "within you" or "in the midst of you" (that is, "among you"). According to the first translation the kingdom is present, in a spiritual way, within the lives and hearts of believers, who experience the power and glory of God within them. According to the second of the translations, probably the more likely of the two, the kingdom is present in the circle of disciples gathered around Jesus. Within the fellowship of Jesus, and thus within the broader Jewish society, too, the kingdom of God already has begun, and the new age already has dawned.

Yet Jesus' proclamation of God's rule does not ignore the future dimension. In the Lord's Prayer Jesus and his followers pray that God's kingdom might come, and that God's will might thereby be accomplished. At the Last Supper, according to Mark 14:25 (and Matt. 26:29, after Mark; cf. also Luke 22:16, 18), Jesus announces that he will not drink wine again until the messianic banquet in the kingdom of God. And in parables like those of Matthew 25, Jesus enjoins his followers to be as watchful as the five wise maidens who kept their lamps burning for the marriage feast—that is, the consummation of the kingdom. For, Jesus warns, a day of crisis and judgment is coming.

*   *   *

When will this world end, and when will the kingdom come? The conviction of Jesus and many believers within the earliest church, I submit, is that the End is near, and the kingdom will come very soon.

To substantiate this suggestion, we turn to Mark 13, and the so-called Synoptic apocalypse. (I shall not undertake here a comparative study of the three versions of this Synoptic apocalypse as found in Mark 13:5–37, Matt. 24:4–36, and Luke 21:8–36, as valuable as that might prove to be. Instead I shall offer only a few comments about the most significant similarities and differences within these three accounts.)

In a manner rather like the visions of the book of Daniel, Mark 13 presents an apocalyptic discourse on present troubles and future salvation. To be sure, for Jesus and for Mark, times had changed since the days of Antiochus Epiphanes, but the issues had not. The oppressors of the people of God still were causing devastation, and only the coming kingdom and Son of Man could provide final hope. Mark was writing about the year 70 C.E.; Antiochus and the Seleucids were long gone, but now Titus and the Romans were about to ruin Jerusalem and the Temple.

After the stage is set by means of Jesus' shocking statement about the destruction of the Temple (13:1–4), the Markan account begins with a woeful list of the sufferings to be experienced. Cold wars and hot wars, along with such cosmic upheavals as earthquakes and famines, will throw the world into commotion, and persecutions and betrayals will make the believer's life a trial (13:5–13). The description of the sufferings experienced during the last days is based upon several Old Testament passages, including 2 Chronicles 15:6, Isaiah 19:2, Micah 7:2, 6, and most importantly several passages in Daniel. By using and updating such texts, the Markan apocalypse proclaims that the final sufferings of this age conform to the promises and patterns revealed by God in the Old Testament.

Such a use of Scripture is even more apparent in Mark 13:14. There Daniel's phrase about the "desolating sacrilege" is taken up as descriptive of the present situation. The fate of the Temple was as precarious as in the days of the Maccabees! In case the reader of Mark missed the allusion to Daniel 9:27, 11:31, and 12:11, the evangelist adds the parenthetical remark "let the reader understand," so that the value of the reference will not be lost. When we turn for a moment to the other Synoptic accounts, we note that Matthew 24:15 outdoes Mark in clarifying this passage, and even mentions Daniel by name. Luke, on the other hand, who is writing well after the destruction of Jerusalem, makes no explicit reference at all to Daniel's "abomination that makes desolate." Instead he includes a statement that seems to be a description of the actual siege and conquest of Jerusalem some years in the past: "But when you see Jerusalem surrounded by armies, then know that its desolation has come near" (21:20). According to Luke, the "desolation" of Daniel and Mark is best interpreted as the fall of Jerusalem back in the year 70. A similar remark further on, in Luke 21:24, speaks of the Jewish captives being led away out of Palestine and into "the nations," while Jerusalem is "trodden down by the Gentiles." This depiction recalls the vivid scene on the Arch of Titus in Rome, where victorious Romans are carrying booty taken from the Jewish Temple and brought to Rome, including a menorah and the table for the showbread.

In the face of this apocalyptic crisis and the grievous tribulation, Mark 13 advises that one ought to run for one's life. "Let those who are in Judea flee to the mountains," says Jesus (Mark 13:14), and let no one turn back or hesitate (13:15–16). The distresses of these final days (13:17–23) will reach a climax when the very fabric of the universe is torn. The sun and moon will be dark (cf. Isa. 13:10; Joel 2:10), and the stars and heavenly powers will fall (cf. Isa. 34:4), predicts Mark 13:24–25. At such a time, when the heavens and earth are going through catastrophic convulsions, the Son of Man will come with the kingdom

(Mark 13:26–27) in a manner reminiscent of Daniel 7:13–14. With power and glory he will usher in the new age, and the chosen people of God will live in peace and salvation.

According to the apocalyptic discourse of Jesus in Mark 13, the final distress and deliverance are imminent. As the parable of the fig tree illustrates (cf. 13:28–29; also 11:12–14, 20–25), the surrounding evidence allows us to recognize apocalyptic times just as we recognize seasonal times. To be sure, Jesus does insist that precise calculations of the day and hour of the End are quite fruitless (Mark 13:32–37), yet at the same time he proclaims that the End is coming quickly. In fact, Mark 13:29 asserts that "he [the Son of Man, or the kingdom—cf. Luke 21:31] is near, at the very gates."

The new age is knocking at the door of the present: this is the message of Jesus and Mark in chapter 13. The message is made that much more emphatic by verse 30: "Truly I say to you, this generation will not pass away before all these things take place." Some brief period of time is required for the proclamation of the gospel, says Mark (13:10). Yet the generation of those alive during Jesus' or Mark's day will live to see the coming of the kingdom (cf. Matt. 24:14). This imminence of the kingdom should function as a real goad to missionary intensity: in Matthew 10:23 Jesus urges the disciples to move quickly from town to town, "for truly, I say to you, you will not have gone through all the towns of Israel before the Son of Man comes." The nearness of the kingdom is also emphasized in Jesus' saying in Mark 9:1: "Truly I say to you, there are some standing here who will not taste death before they see that the kingdom of God has come with power." According to the most obvious and straightforward way of understanding this text, Jesus announced that some of his followers would experience the consummation of the kingdom during their lifetimes. Indeed, "the kingdom of God coming with power" can hardly be taken in any other way, and Matthew also understood the expression to mean precisely that (cf. Matt. 16:28: he revises Mark to read "the Son of Man coming in his kingdom," that is, at the end of this age). Thus, the kingdom of God, already present in the ministry of Jesus, will manifest itself soon.

If Mark and his apocalypse proclaim the imminence of the kingdom, another believer of "this generation" who anticipated that the End was at hand was the apostle Paul. In what was probably his first New Testament letter, 1 Thessalonians, Paul dealt with a problem facing the church in the middle of the century. Christians were still awaiting the End, in eager expectation that they would see the kingdom soon; but it simply did not come. As those Christians waited, some of their loved ones died. So the believers who remained alive were fearful that these loved ones, since they had died during the waiting period, might not be able to experience the coming new age that had not come soon enough for them. To reassure them, Paul wrote to the Thessalonians that their dead relatives and friends would participate as fully in the kingdom as those who were alive at the end time. And in his choice of words he intimates that he, as well as many of his readers, would live to see that day! He writes, using the first-person plural, that "we who are alive, who are left until the coming of the Lord," shall join with "those who have fallen asleep," in the joy of the new age (4:15; cf. 4:17).

A few years later, in writing to the Corinthians, Paul expressed similar sentiments. In 1 Corinthians 7 Paul gives counsel concerning life-style and marriage, and among his suggestions he includes the advice that men and women should stay just as they are without turning over too many new leaves in their lives. Gentiles should not bother getting circumcised, and Jews should not try to obliterate their marks of circumcision; slaves need not bother getting emancipated; married people should not seek divorce, nor single people marriage. The rationale for this rather strange advice is that there simply is not enough time left in this age to worry about such mundane matters. "The appointed time has grown very short" (7:29), writes Paul, and "the form of this world is passing away" (7:31). So why get embroiled in worldly hassles if this world is destined to reach an imminent end? Obviously, most Christians since the time of Paul have not followed the advice given here in 1 Corinthians.

To sum up: Jesus announced that the kingdom was near at hand, Paul stated that the time of the present world was growing short, and Mark proclaimed that the current generation would experience both "the desolating sacrilege" in the holy city of Jerusalem and the coming of the kingdom and the Son of Man with consummate power. Many people in that apocalyptic generation of Christians believed, along with Jesus, Paul, and Mark, that the new age would come very soon. Yet their generation came and went, along with dozens of generations since. The End has not yet come, and since that first century Christians have reflected again and again about the kingdom of God and the end of the world.

*   *   *

One New Testament author who tries to cope with this issue of the delay of the coming kingdom, sometimes called the delay of the parousia (that is, the second "coming" of Christ), is Luke. Luke's work is actually a two-volume one. Luke and Acts belong together, as the two-part story of Jesus and the early church. As the plot unfolds in Luke-Acts, the action moves from the backwoods region of Galilee to Jerusalem and on to the mission of the church throughout this northeastern Mediterranean world. In fact, we may take the very existence of a book like Acts as evidence for the delay of the parousia. Were the End truly near, the emphasis upon an open-ended mission of the church "in Jerusalem and in all Judea and Samaria and to the end of the earth" (Acts 1:8) would be impossible. The conclusion of Acts, showing Paul in Rome, "preaching the kingdom of God and teaching about the Lord Jesus Christ quite openly and unhindered" (28:31), provides an uplifting conclusion to the story, and an encouraging stimulus for the reader to continue the worldwide witness of the church.

In his Gospel Luke shows how he adjusts to the delay of the parousia by revising Mark in subtle but notable ways. Let us consider a few examples. To begin with, Mark's summary of Jesus' apocalyptic proclamation of the imminent kingdom, "The kingdom of God is at hand; repent . . ." (1:15), is missing in Luke, who has only general statements about preaching in Galilee (4:14–15) and teaching in the synagogue of Nazareth (4:16–30). Again, in the Lukan version of the apocalyptic discourse, where the Markan Jesus warns against messianic pretenders who "will come in my name, saying, 'I am he!'" (13:6), Luke cautions also against those who claim "The time is at hand!" (21:8). In other words, Luke specifically opposes an apocalyptic approach like Mark's, which emphasizes the imminent advent of the kingdom! Elsewhere in Luke's Gospel the same point is made: the parable of the pounds in chapter 19 was told, it is said, to help refute the conviction "that the kingdom of God was to appear immediately" (19:11). It is true that the expectation of a future kingdom is by no means absent from Luke, but stress is placed on the present time as the period of the missionary witness of the church to the whole world.

For Luke, as well as for other authors of the later New Testament books, the matter that is of central concern is the place and task of the church on earth. The apocalyptic fervor of the middle portion of the century was a thing of the past. The fall of Jerusalem had happened some time before and, traumatic as it was, the church and the world had persevered through that tribulation. Now, around the end of the century, the church was gearing up and getting organized for the long march that lay ahead. To be sure, neoapocalyptic enthusiasts would arise fairly frequently during the church's history to announce the Second Coming as the imminent hope for believers living through times of uncertainty, violence, and oppression. During the last decade of the first Christian century, for instance, the persecutions of the Emperor Domitian prompted the composition of the book of Revelation, with its proclamation of hope that good would triumph over evil, and the Lamb from heaven would defeat yet another apocalyptic beast from the watery abyss.

Thus Luke and the other New Testament writers faced the realities of the present and the future in various ways. Yet they each sought to respond to the issues and demands of their day by means of a timely proclamation of the good news. There is hope in the present moment, and promise in the unfolding future of God's reign.

D. S. Russell's handy book *Between the Testaments* (Philadelphia: Fortress, 1965) includes good material introducing the Jewish apocalyptic movement. For more substantial presentations several books and monographs are available. Three of the best are Russell's book, *The Method and Message of Jewish Apocalyptic* (Philadelphia: Westminster, 1964); Paul D. Hanson, *The Dawn of Apocalyptic* (Philadelphia: Fortress, 1975); and Paul S. Minear, *New Testament Apocalyptic* (Nashville: Abingdon, 1981). On the controversy over the date and authorship of Daniel, see Brevard S. Childs, *Introduction to the Old Testament as Scripture* (Philadelphia: Fortress, 1979), pp. 608–23.

For an analysis of the Hellenistic period, and the relationships and interactions of Judaism and Hellenism during this period, see F. E. Peters, *The Harvest of Hellenism* (New York: Simon and Schuster, 1970), especially pp. 222–308; also W. W. Tarn and G. T. Griffith, *Hellenistic Civilization* (Cleveland: World, 1961); and Martin Hengel, *Judaism and Hellenism* (Philadelphia: Fortress, 1974), 2 vols.

The delay of the parousia is such a dominant theme in New Testament literature that discussions of it are to be found almost wherever one looks. Several of the books cited in the bibliographical notes appended to previous chapters contain useful comments (i.e., Kümmel, Perrin, and the commentaries). Perhaps most valuable is the brief essay on "Eschatology of the New Testament" in the Supplementary Volume of *The Interpreter's Dictionary of the Bible* (Nashville: Abingdon, 1976), pp. 271–77, with its ample bibliography.

7
HOW BAD WAS
GOOD FRIDAY?

The scandal and glory of the crucifixion

IN contrast to the mahogany crosses and silver crucifixes that today decorate church sanctuaries and grace human necks, the ancient cross was not an attractive object of art. It was a gallows, and yet more than a gallows, since it was not only an instrument of execution but also a device of torture. Hence death by crucifixion was a method of execution reserved for the very worst of criminals, or even for slaves. In particular, those who had committed crimes against the state might be candidates for crucifixion, for this was a specifically Roman means of capital punishment. The two "robbers" (Mark 15:27) crucified along with Jesus probably were revolutionaries who had been involved in an insurrection against the Roman forces of occupation. Their crucifixion would be a good object-lesson for others who similarly might be plotting a rebellion against the Roman rule of Palestine.

Death by crucifixion often was death by exposure and dehydration; the scream "I'm thirsty!" (John 19:28) must have been hideously common. The convicted criminal was tied or nailed to a gallows, to be exposed to the elements until dead. Usually such a death was an agonizing one, slow in coming. Several days could pass as the body of the victim underwent the torments of the heat, the cold, the sun, and the wind. Military guards were stationed at the site of the execution to ensure that no friend or relative would come by to release the victim from the cross.

An archeological discovery in Palestine has given us additional information about the gruesome means of crucifixion. When a victim was nailed to a cross, one nail was driven through both of the heels, with the legs either together off to one side, or spread with knees apart. The nails holding the arms were not driven through the soft palms, but rather through the wrist, where the nails would be more likely to hold. A small seat or shelf most likely was used to help support the weight of the crucified person. Otherwise the victim might die too quickly and too easily.

Jesus of Nazareth was delivered up for such an execution. As an enthusiast for the kingdom of God, he went from Galilee to Jerusalem in order to celebrate the Passover and proclaim the kingdom in "the city of the great King" (Matt. 5:35). He entered Jerusalem triumphantly with all the messianic overtones that could accompany such a patriotic demonstration, but the road he had chosen led to his death. After he shared a last meal with his disciples, Jesus was handed over by one of his own followers, Judas Iscariot, and arrested by the authorities. Charged with blasphemy by the Jewish court (Mark 14:53–72 and parallels) and with political sedition by the Romans (Mark 15:1–5 and parallels), Jesus was condemned by the Roman Procurator Pontius Pilate to death by crucifixion. Those around him mocked him about his plight, and the inscription on the cross, "The king of the Jews" (Mark 15:26 and parallels), gave ample warning of how the Romans dealt with those who had royal pretensions. As was their custom, the soldiers stationed there cast lots to determine who should take possession of the victim's clothing (Mark 15:24 and parallels). Mercifully, Jesus' death was comparatively quick in coming. Although he refused to drink the wine laced with drugs to dull the pain (Mark 15:23; Matt. 27:34), he lingered only six hours after being nailed to the gallows. Thus Jesus died, in humility and ignominy, as a convicted political criminal crucified outside Jerusalem on the hill Golgotha.

Jesus' bold and independent ministry had made him just too many enemies. Some of the Jewish leaders were suspicious of his popularity with the common people, while others hated him for his potent and critical words about the proper life of Torah. The Sadducees, who directed Temple worship, were incensed by his offensive behavior in "cleansing" the Jewish sanctuary (Mark 11:15–19 and parallels). His friends and acquaintances did not inspire confidence, either. He became involved with wild-eyed apocalypticists like John the Baptist's people, he associated with political agitators from among the Zealots, and he spent time with tax collectors, prostitutes, and sinners. He even recited a parable in which a despised Samaritan is spoken of more highly than a Jewish priest and a Levite (Luke 10:29–37)! Furthermore, his commitment to the kingdom of God, and the explicit or implicit suggestions about his own role in the kingdom, made him a threat, especially in the eyes of the Romans, to national security.

In short, to many different people of his day, Jesus had become an irritant and a public nuisance: he needed to be eliminated.

In his teaching ministry Jesus once had said, "From the days of John the Baptist until now the kingdom of heaven has suffered violence, and violent people take it by force" (Matt. 11:12). So it had happened with the Baptist, who was executed by the powers that be. Now Jesus, too, was made to suffer the same sort of violence at the hands of the "violent people," and yet he faithfully followed God and God's kingdom to the cross.

*   *   *

Good Friday might easily be termed "Bad Friday," for it was a day of violence, shame, and infamy. The earliest extant depiction of the crucifixion, given in a graffito from Rome, shows what people in the ancient world thought of the cross. Far from representing the crucified Christ in victory, as is the case with later works of art, this graffito ridicules the very concept of a crucified person being a savior. It pictures an individual praying to an ass-headed figure on a cross, and includes a caption mocking Christian faith: "Alexamenos worships God."

Paul, too, acknowledges that the Christian proclamation of "Christ crucified" is offensive. "We preach Christ crucified," admits Paul, "a stumbling block [or scandal] to Jews and folly to Gentiles" (1 Cor. 1:23). Jews want "signs," or mighty manifestations of the divine presence, Paul writes, and Greeks pursue the wisdom of philosophical inquiry. Thus for the former the crucifixion is weak and shameful, and for the latter it is irrational and absurd. But this Christian gospel of scandal and foolishness, Paul quickly adds, is both powerful and wise to those who believe. With a nice turn of phrase Paul concludes that this same "Christ crucified," who is the content of his preaching, is "Christ the power of God and wisdom of God" to Jewish and Greek believers. "For the foolishness of God is wiser than people, and the weakness of God is stronger than people" (1:24–25).

Paul's proclamation of the crucifixion as the saving event of a "Good" Friday presupposes a Christian interpretation that stresses the positive place and significance of the death of Jesus. In the introduction to the Pauline creed of 1 Corinthians 15, Paul concedes that he had been instructed in the essentials of such Christian interpretation, and had made these points the core of his own proclamation: "I delivered to you as of first importance what I also received" (15:3). The first item in the creed highlights the crucifixion, and does so in an interesting fashion: "Christ died for our sins *in accordance with the scriptures."* As we may conclude on the basis of this Pauline or pre-Pauline creed, from the earliest years of the church Christians professed that the execution of Jesus was by no means a meaningless tragedy, or a more-or-less random accident of history. Rather, it was a crucial part of the plan of God. These earliest of Christians related the crucifixion to the Old Testament promises of God, and thus proclaimed that the death of Jesus, with all its pain and anguish, took place "in accordance with the scriptures."

Paul also ties the crucifixion to texts from the Old Testament. In Galatians, for instance, he grants that crucifixion is an accursed affair, but suggests that the curse is part of the plan of God. After all, "it is written, 'Cursed be every one who hangs on a tree' " (Gal. 3:13, quoting Deut. 21:23). By taking our curse upon himself, "Christ redeemed us from the curse of the law." In such a fashion Paul takes the edge off the curse by preaching that it, too, is entirely within the will and design of God for our salvation.

Such interpretations of the crucifixion allow Christians to move past the stumbling block of the cross and to understand it in a new, more glorious light. If Paul illustrates a concern for setting the death of Jesus within the context of the Old Testament, the New Testament Gospels show much more of an interest in linking the specifics of Old Testament "passions" with the passion of Jesus.

We turn, then, to the four Gospels and their passion narratives.

If there is one overwhelming impression left by the passion narratives, it is this: their authors were convinced that Jesus' death was in fulfillment of prophecy. So convinced were they of this matter that they used not only traditions about Jesus' death but also statements from the Old Testament prophets to enrich their accounts of the crucifixion. In this way the Old Testament aided them as they composed their accounts of the crucifixion as saving event.

Consequently, we should note a few of the many allusions to and quotations of the Old Testament in the four accounts of the crucifixion itself (Mark 15:22–41; Matt. 27:33–56; Luke 23:33–49; John 19:17–37). Since Psalm 22, a "suffering psalm" with a triumphant conclusion, was particularly important for the interpretation of Jesus' execution, we shall focus upon the use of this Old

Testament chapter in the four passion narratives. Just as Psalm 22 opens with the cry to God, "My God, my God, why have you forsaken me?" (22:1), so also Jesus in Mark 15:34 and Matthew 27:46 screams the same anguished cry. In Luke's passion account, however, Jesus does not speak these moving words. Instead, his final words are "Father, into your hands I commit my spirit" (23:46), a quotation from Psalm 31:5, which is followed by a most appropriate line: "you have redeemed me, O Lord, faithful God." Again, as Psalm 22:7 mentions the mockery of the poet's foes and the wagging of the heads, so also Mark 15:29 and Matthew 27:39 refer to both the derision of the passers-by and the wagging of their heads. Matthew 27:43 even puts Psalm 22:8 on the mocking lips of the Jewish leaders! Again, Psalm 22:16 declares that the evildoers "have pierced my hands and feet," a statement that would be generally reminiscent of crucifixion. And once again, Psalm 22:18, consisting of two parallel lines,

> they divide my garments among them,
> and for my raiment they cast lots,

is reflected in Mark 15:24, Matthew 27:35, Luke 23:34, and John 19:23–24. In John's account, however, a distinction is made between the division of the garments in general and the tunic of Jesus, with lots being cast only for the latter specific article of clothing. Here John, in contrast to the Synoptics, interprets the parallel lines of Psalm 22 literally, and so comes up with two procedures for the disposal of the clothing—just as Matthew did with the donkeys, which we discussed in Chapter Five.

Other examples could be cited, but the matter should be clear enough from the preceding. The authors of the passion narratives self-consciously sought to relate the crucifixion of Jesus to the Old Testament. Now it certainly is possible that some of the similarities between the passion of Jesus and the Old Testament passages go back to the historical crucifixion of Jesus. For instance, it may be that Jesus, as a devout Jew, cried out the words of Psalm 22 in his agony on the cross. Perhaps this psalm, more than any other, might come welling out of the heart of one like the crucified Jesus. Nevertheless, it is apparent that Old Testament texts such as Psalm 22 also played a more creative and formative role in the passion accounts of the New Testament Gospels. In particular, the details of the crucifixion are reinterpreted and refined on the basis of the authoritative texts of the Old Testament.

As a result, the passion narratives and the four Gospels transcend the horror of Jesus as a crucified criminal, and see the death of Jesus in a broader, salvific context.

A later account in Luke of a resurrection appearance on the Emmaus road (24:13–35) describes a mysterious stranger also telling the story of the crucified Jesus and relating this story to the Old Testament Scriptures. Verses 25–26 have the stranger—the risen Christ—utter these sentences (appropriate for the present discussion): "O foolish people, and slow of heart to believe all that the prophets have spoken! Was it not necessary that the Christ should suffer these things and enter into his glory?" Here, then, is the gist of the accounts of Jesus' passion: it was necessary. It was necessary that Jesus suffer and die, the evangelists proclaim, to fulfill God's will and God's word. Besides, suffering and death are not the conclusion of the matter. As Luke asserts, glory awaits Jesus, for the crucified one is to be exalted.

*   *   *

If any one New Testament Gospel could be entitled the "gospel of glory and exaltation," without a doubt it would be the Gospel of John. Since the next and last chapter will consider the glory of the resurrected Christ in the Gospels, this theme should not detain us here. Rather, in mentioning John as the gospel of glory, I am thinking particularly of the way in which John contends that the crucifixion itself was a moment of glory for Jesus.

The overarching outline of Jesus' career as interpreted in the Gospel of John differs considerably from that of the Synoptic Gospels. John 1 and 17 give us the most significant hints of John's perspective on Jesus. According to the hymn to the Word in John 1:1–18, Jesus' career begins with creation itself. "In the beginning was the Word," writes John. Thus he echoes Genesis 1:1, and in fact provides his own—Christian—creation account. In the beginning the divine Word exists: he is active in creation (1:3), and disseminates life and light that cannot be overcome. Following the prosaic interlude concerning John the Baptist (1:6–8), the chapter resumes its hymning of the Word by describing how the Word, Christ, comes down to earth. He enters the world as its fashioner and its enlightener, yet he is unknown, unrecognized, even by his own people (1:9–11). Still, some do believe in him, and they receive power and partake of his fullness

(1:12–13, 16). For "the Word became flesh," and dwelt (or tabernacled) among humans, and "we have beheld his glory, glory as of the only Son from the Father" (1:14). Thus Christ, the glorious Word from God and emissary from above, makes God known to people on earth (1:18).

Most of the rest of John's Gospel describes the specifics in the story of the incarnate Word. Christ the Word performs signs as marvelous indicators of his divine power. Yet even these signs are reinterpreted in majestic, mystical discourses that function as the revelation of a divine being. As one sent by the Father (a common phrase in John), Jesus the Word communicates God to those who would know truth. But the resistance of the world grows, and eventually culminates in the crucifixion of Jesus. Even in abuse and death, however, the exalted Jesus of the Gospel of John is an authoritative figure who is in charge of his own destiny. He knows what will happen to him in his passion (18:4); the soldiers sent to arrest him collapse in the presence of his power (18:6); he is able to care for his disciples by sending them away (18:8–9), while he himself voluntarily determines to "drink the cup which the Father has given" (18:11); and he finally emerges as the one truly in command in the presence of the Jewish officials (18:20–24) and Pilate (18:33–38). At one point the Johannine Jesus even snaps back at an irate Pilate, "You would have no power over me unless it had been given to you from above" (19:11).

John 17, Jesus' high-priestly prayer, is actually a commentary on the passion of Jesus. Jesus opens his prayer by saying, "Father, the hour has come; glorify your Son that the Son may glorify you, since you have given him power over all flesh, to give eternal life to all whom you have given him" (17:1–2). "The hour" is a term peculiar to the Gospel of John, and commonly designates the time culminating in Jesus' death (see also 7:30; 8:20; 12:23; 12:27; 13:1). In John 17 the hour of suffering and death, however, is said to be a time of glory—glory for Jesus and glory for the Father as well! Eternal life is attained for his own, and Jesus himself returns in death up to the presence of God once again, to experience (as he prays in John 17:5) "the glory which I had with you before the world was made." The cycle of his career thus is complete. The cosmic Christ, though crucified, returns back to glory once again, to resume his position as the divine Word "in the bosom of the Father" (1:18). Thus, in John's proclamation of the good news of Jesus, the cross has become a bridge to glory.

*   *   *

Frequently it is maintained that the Gospel of John, in its interpretation of the exalted Savior, moves in the same thought-world as early Christian Gnostics, those mystics who stressed the importance of the knowledge, or *gnosis,* of God, and preached Jesus as the revealer of such wonderful, life-giving knowledge. As we compare the Gospel of John with Gnostic gospels and other Gnostic documents, we immediately notice the similarity of their point of view. Like John, the Gnostic gospels make dualistic use of concepts like light and darkness, or life and death (cf. John 1:5; 11:25–26). As John also does, the Gnostic sources emphasize Jesus as a descending-ascending redeemer, who comes down from the glory of God, lives for a time upon the earth, utters profound teachings in "I am" self-predications and revelatory discourses, and finally returns once again to the glory and fullness of God.

A good example of this sort of Gnostic interpretation of Jesus occurs in a short work from the Nag Hammadi library, the Letter of Peter to Philip. In this text Christ is pictured on the Mount of Olives delivering a long discourse on topics having to do with salvation. He opens a part of his speech with an "I am" statement about the "fullness" of God: "Now concerning the fullness, it is I." Jesus then proceeds to discuss the main moments in his career in terms reminiscent of John 1. He was sent down from above, put on a "mortal model" (that is, some sort of body), but was not recognized by the powers of the world (cf. John 1:10). When he spoke with his own (cf. John 1:11–12), however, they hearkened to him, and were given authority and power, so that they, too, "became fullness" (cf. John 1:16).

Some Christian Gnostic texts, in their desire to proclaim a truly divine Christ, maintain that so exalted a being as Christ could not possibly have a real body of flesh as we humans do. He is too divine, too glorious for that. Christians making these claims are called "docetists" (from the Greek verb *dokeo,* "seem"), because they believe that the heavenly Christ only "seemed" to have a fleshly body. And if Christ did not have a real body of flesh, then two conclusions may be drawn: he was not fully human, and so he could not suffer and die as human beings do.

Accordingly, Gnostic sources sometimes proclaim a docetic Jesus who undergoes a docetic crucifixion. For such Gnostics the pain of the cross is eliminated entirely. As Jesus puts it in one such text, "I did not really die, but only in appearance." Some Gnostic texts say that a corpse of flesh was nailed to the tree; others state that a substitute victim, Simon of Cyrene, was crucified instead of Jesus. In either case Jesus escapes the disgrace of the cross, and stands above it all in heavenly grandeur. Several Gnostic documents even portray him surveying the scene at the crucifixion, and laughing at the stupidity of those who think they can execute the Lord of glory.

To such docetists of the past and present the Gospel of John speaks clearly and decisively: "the Word became flesh" (1:14). For John, like the Christian Gnostics, the hour of crucifixion is the hour of glory. Yet John refuses to succumb to the anesthetized gospel of a laughing Jesus. The Johannine Jesus is the divine Word who hangs crucified in the flesh, and in the mystery of this message lies John's special power.

For fine, brief analyses of the New Testament passion narratives, see Rudolf Bultmann, *The History of the Synoptic Tradition* (New York: Harper & Row, 1963), pp. 262–84; and the article "Passion Narrative" in the Supplementary Volume of *The Interpreter's Dictionary of the Bible* (Nashville: Abingdon, 1976), pp. 643–45. In the same volume the entry on "Method of Crucifixion" gives a description, sketches, and bibliography relating to the recent archeological discovery of the skeleton of a crucified person from a tomb in first-century Jerusalem. The place of the death of Jesus in the Gospel of John, especially John 17, is delineated in a short book by Ernst Käsemann, *The Testament of Jesus* (Philadelphia: Fortress, 1968).

The discussion of the crucifixion in Gnostic sources is based in part upon my article "Jesus in the Nag Hammadi Library" published in *The Reformed Journal* 29 (1979): 14–18. The translations from the Letter of Peter to Philip are taken from my book *The Letter of Peter to Philip* (Chico, Calif.: Scholars, 1981). The figure of the Gnostic Jesus laughing at the foolish authorities has inspired the title of a good book by John Dart, *The Laughing Savior* (New York: Harper & Row, 1976). I might also mention that the Quran *sura* 4 has a description of the crucifixion that is similar to that of the Gnostics. See Tor Andrae, *Mohammed: The Man and His Faith* (New York: Harper & Row, 1960), pp. 112–13; Geoffrey Parrinder, *Jesus in the Quran* (New York: Oxford Univ. Press, 1977), pp. 105–21.

The Roman graffito of the crucifixion is published in Michael Gough, *The Early Christians* (London: Thames and Hudson, 1961), pp. 83–84.

8

HOW DID
JESUS ARISE?

The resurrection of Christ and Christians

"HE has risen." In these words of the white-robed young man in Mark 16:6 we confront the common profession of early Christian preachers of the gospel. The gospel indeed is *good* news: the crucified Jesus becomes the risen Lord.

The earliest New Testament discussions of the resurrection are to be found in Paul. In the ancient creed of 1 Corinthians 15 Paul confesses, with those who so confessed before him, "that he [namely Christ] was raised on the third day in accordance with the scriptures" (15:4). Like his crucifixion, Jesus' resurrection also is said to be part of the divine plan. In the next verses Paul furnishes a list of those who witnessed the resurrection, who claimed that the risen Christ had appeared to them. The list begins with Peter, who often is described in Christian sources as the first of the disciples to experience Christ after his resurrection. Various other witnesses are recorded, including James (probably James the Just, the brother of Jesus, whose encounter with the risen Christ is described in an apocryphal gospel). Last of all Paul also mentions himself as a witness. Paul's self-effacing words in 1 Corinthians 15:8–11 must not be understood merely to indicate modesty about himself and his status as witness to the resurrection. Rather, Paul seeks to accomplish a couple of important things in these verses. First, he speaks to the issue that he, a relatively recent convert and now a Christian missionary, once upon a time had been vehemently opposed to the church. As Paul writes autobiographically in Galatians 1:13, "I persecuted the church of God violently and tried to destroy it" (cf. Acts 8:3; 9:1–2, 21; 22:4–5). Second, Paul suggests that his own position as witness to the resurrection and as apostle of Christ should be seen from the vantage point of his gospel of grace: he is what he is by God's grace (15:10). Although Paul exclaims that he has been a more diligent worker for the church than anyone, he quickly reverses himself, in his typical way of writing (cf., for instance, Gal. 4:9), by adding, "though it was not I, but the grace of God which is with me."

The rest of 1 Corinthians 15 deals with two questions about the resurrection of believers and also, by implication, the resurrection of Jesus. The first question is put rhetorically by Paul: "How can some of you say that there is no resurrection of the dead?" (15:12). This denial of the resurrection of the dead (and thus also, Paul warns, the resurrection of Christ) was not just the expression of doubt on the part of unbelieving skeptics, for the question is addressed by Paul to Christian believers in the church at Corinth! Rather, this denial seems to be directed toward the idea of a future resurrection of dead people. Apparently some Christians in Corinth were positing that resurrection is a thing of the past, something that already has happened in the Christian life. Such a doctrine certainly makes some sense, doesn't it: the Christian realizes the new life in the here and now, as she or he dies with Christ and also rises to spiritual completion with Christ. Thus, these Christians conclude, the most reasonable way of speaking about the resurrection is not as something that happens to the dead at a future date, but instead as the transformation that already has taken place for the baptized, born-again believer.

We know of some early Christians, besides these Corinthians, who held to this interpretation of the resurrection. In 2 Timothy 2:16–18, for example, we have a polemical characterization of Hymenaeus and Philetus, who, the author states, "have swerved from the truth by holding that the resurrection is past already." And now, in the texts of the Nag Hammadi library, we discover other Christians who make similar claims. In the Gnostic Treatise on Resurrection the author proclaims the supreme reality of the resurrection: "It is no illusion, but it is truth. Indeed, it is more fitting to say that the world is an illusion, rather than the resurrection which has come into being through our Lord the Savior, Jesus Christ." Moreover, this resurrection, this truest of truths, is not relegated to the end time, but has become a spiritual reality now. As the author of the treatise writes, "already you have the resurrection."

Paul agrees with such early Christians that the believer dies and rises with Christ, but parts company with them concerning the time of the resurrection. On the one hand, Paul declares that in baptism one identifies oneself intimately with Christ. In his words, which bring to mind the clothing taken off and put on in early baptismal ceremonies, those who "were baptized into Christ have put on Christ" (Gal. 3:27), and this spiritual clothing transforms one's life in remarkable ways (3:28). To be sure, Paul understands baptism to be a death experience, so that the believer has been crucified and buried with Christ (Rom. 6:3–4; Gal. 2:20). On the other hand, while he admits that the new life of Christ has already begun, he insists that the completion, the perfection of this new life must await the future resurrection. It is significant that Paul consistently uses the future tense to describe the resurrection. In Romans 6:5, for example, he states that "if *we have been united* with him in a death like his, *we shall certainly be united* with him in a resurrection like his."

We have died, we shall rise: this is Paul's way of presenting his gospel. Paul is too much of an apocalyptic thinker to be content with a salvation fully realized in the present situation. He wants to preach hope, and "hope that is seen," he contends in Romans 8:24, "is not hope." For Paul the hope in the future resurrection means that one can live through the present pains and imperfections with a conviction that the future will be glorious. He sums up these sentiments splendidly in a well-known verse, Romans 8:18: "I consider that the sufferings of this present time are not worth comparing with the glory that is to be revealed to us."

The second question about the resurrection in 1 Corinthians 15 occurs in verse 35: "How are the dead raised?" To this he immediately adds a companion question: "With what kind of body do they come?" Paul and the Apostles' Creed concur in the confession that the resurrection is a resurrection of the body, but Paul is very careful in his description of this body. It is clear that the resurrected body, according to Paul, is quite different from the human body as we think of it. This new body is imperishable, glorious, powerful, spiritual (15:42–44)! So peculiar is Paul's use of the word "body" here in 1 Corinthians 15 that he goes to the trouble to explain his vocabulary: "If there is a physical body, there is also a spiritual body" (15:44). Lest his readers be tempted to revert back to a mundane understanding of the physical, fleshly body, Paul closes the paragraph with a clear assertion: "flesh and blood cannot inherit the kingdom of God, nor does the perishable inherit the imperishable" (15:50).

Hence Paul preaches a spiritual resurrection. His offbeat use of the term "body" ought not to confuse us. The resurrection body, he maintains, is not a body of flesh and bones and blood. Rather, it is something glorious and bright; and Paul even finds it appropriate in this context to discuss different kinds of glory (15:40–41).

We may extrapolate from this spiritual resurrection to the resurrection of Jesus. If Christ's resurrection is the pattern, the "first fruits" (15:23), for the resurrection of believers, and if believers will experience "a resurrection like his" (Rom. 6:5), then his resurrection also may be described as a spiritual event. This point is made definitively in 1 Corinthians 15:45: "Thus it is written, 'The first man Adam became a living being'; the last Adam became a life-giving spirit." By means of these two parallel statements, Paul moves from the first man of Genesis (the scriptural citation is from Gen. 2:7) to the final Man—that is, Christ—of the Christian gospel. Paul observes that Christ becomes a life-giving spirit. He is life-giving because of the salvation he works, and he is spirit because that is what he becomes in his resurrection. For Paul, Christ arose as a spirit.

Christian Gnostics, with their propensity for the spiritual and the mystical, naturally appreciated the idea of a glorious, spiritual resurrection. Gnostic literature abounds with examples of such an interpretation of the resurrection of Christ and Christians, but we shall consider only a few representative lines from the Letter of Peter to Philip. There the risen Christ appears, but not with any sort of fleshly body. Instead, he appears as a disembodied light and voice—the light of glory and the voice of revelation. The glory of this spiritual occasion is highlighted by the "theological landscape": it takes place on a mountain, Olivet. In fact, so glorious and bright is the appearance that "the mountain shone from the sight of him who appeared." The voice rings out, and utters heavenly words of revelation, including an initial self-predication: "I am Jesus Christ who is with you for ever."

*   *   *

Like Paul, the New Testament Gospels emphasize the overwhelming significance of the resurrection. At the same time, they each approach the resurrection of Jesus in their own manner. Mark 16:1–8 depicts the empty tomb, as do the other evangelists (Matt. 28:1–8; Luke 24:1–12; John 20:1–13). Mark has a young man in white at the tomb (16:5–7), Matthew an impressive apocalyptic angel (28:2–7), Luke two men in bright clothing (24:4–7), and John two angels in white (20:11–13). Mark includes the promise of the imminent return and appearance of Jesus in Galilee (16:7), but has no accounts of actual appearances of the risen Christ. This displeased some ancient scribes, who added several longer endings to Mark in various manuscripts. These endings, sometimes printed as footnotes in modern translations of the New Testament, contain various edifying stories, including appearance accounts derived from the other Gospels. Matthew has two brief appearance stories: the appearance to the women (28:9–10), and the so-called Great Commission, in which the risen Jesus stands in majesty upon a mountain in Galilee (28:16–20).

Luke has a different series of appearance stories: on the road to Emmaus (24:13–35, with a reference to an appearance to Simon in 24:34), and to the eleven disciples (24:36–49). Unlike the other Synoptics, Luke specifies that all the appearances of the resurrected Jesus took place around Jerusalem in Judea, a factor that allows Luke to proceed more neatly along his geographical route from Galilee to Jerusalem, and outward from there toward Rome and "the end of the earth" (Acts 1:8). Luke's revision of Mark's account allows him to avoid the issue of the Galilean locale for the resurrection appearances. Mark 16:7 describes the youth at the tomb saying, "But go, tell his disciples and Peter that *he is going before you to Galilee;* there you will see him, as he told you." Luke, however, modifies this in 24:6, where his men say, "Remember how he told you *while he was still in Galilee....*" Later Luke even presents Jesus commanding his disciples to stay in Jerusalem until the Lukan Pentecost (Acts 1:4). In addition, Luke is the only evangelist to add an account of the ascension of Jesus (Luke 24:50–53; Acts 1:9–11).

Lastly, the Gospel of John portrays Jesus appearing to Mary Magdalene near the tomb (20:14–18), and to the assembled disciples upon a couple of occasions (20:19–29). At one of these assemblies the Holy Spirit is breathed by Jesus onto the disciples, in the Johannine "Pentecost" (20:21–23). An additional chapter, John 21, describes yet another appearance to the disciples, now by the Sea of Tiberias (that is, the Sea of Galilee).

Luke 24:36–43 is especially important for our purposes. In these verses the risen Christ certainly has an enigmatic, even glorious aspect. After all, he does startle the disciples by materializing in the midst of them. At the same time, however, the resurrected Christ has an ordinary, down-to-earth, human quality that overshadows the glory. On the road to Emmaus he looks like any other traveler, and is recognized only when he is met in worship (24:30–31, 35). In the appearance to the eleven, Luke has Christ say to the disciples, "See my hands and my feet, that it is I myself; handle me, and see; for a spirit has not flesh and bones as you see that I have" (24:39). He even takes a fish and eats it (24:41–43), so human is he. According to Luke, then, in marked contrast to Paul, the risen Christ is not a spirit, but rather has flesh and bones.

The response of the disciples to the sudden appearance of Jesus in Luke 24:37 may provide a clue to help us understand Luke's intentions. The disciples, he writes, were afraid, and "supposed that they saw a spirit." In exegeting this passage I would suggest that the reaction of the eleven disciples in about the year 30 is not Luke's only concern, nor even his chief concern, in these verses. Luke is also concerned about Christian disciples and followers during his own day, and about what his own contemporaries were saying regarding the risen Christ. Near the end of the first century some Christians, perhaps Gnostic Christians, were indeed professing, more adamantly than Paul had done years before, that Jesus arose and appeared as a spirit. In opposition to this profession Luke voiced his own interpretation of the appearances of the resurrected Christ.

It is not that Luke refuses to show Christ appearing in heavenly glory. In his three accounts of the appearance to Paul on the Damascus road (Acts 9:1–22; 22:4–16; and 26:9–18; cf. also Gal. 1:12, 15–16; 2 Cor. 12:2–4), Luke pictures Jesus in magnificent spiritual majesty. All the typical features of such an account, as outlined above, are present in Acts. A bright light flashes from heaven and a voice questions Paul. Those with Paul, however, are not privy to the vision, and hence are not aware of the presence of Christ. (In Acts 9:7 they hear the voice but see no one; in Acts 22:9 they see the light but hear no voice.) The might and glory of the experience are so great that Paul falls down and is temporarily blinded by the appearance. Furthermore, the voice speaks forth in an "I am" fashion: "I am Jesus, whom you are persecuting" (9:5, with variations elsewhere).

Luke is willing to retain such a glorious account of Christ's appearance to Paul because of what it is. It is Paul's vision, and is not a part of the foundational period of the church before Pentecost. During that key period of time between the resurrection and the ascension Luke's Christ was founding his church, and the foundation needed to be firm and sure. Luke must have been a good, insightful churchman who had his feet firmly planted on the ground. He realized that for the church to survive in the world it had to be well established within history. An ecclesiastical organization built upon experiences as ephemeral and other-worldly as glorious visions and encounters with a disembodied spirit would not do for Luke. So Luke, in his interpretation and proclamation, presents a risen Christ who grounds his church upon the strong, solid, tangible stuff of history.

*   *   *

In their own ways, the New Testament evangelists all agree with Paul that the resurrection of Christ to new life is indispensable for Christian faith. As Paul phrases it in 1 Corinthians 15, without the resurrection faith is futile and Christians are pitiable. That is to say, without the living Christ the Christian gospel is hollow and lifeless, an archeological curiosity of an apocalyptic age long past.

The proclamation "he is risen" reverberates through the New Testament and through the centuries of Christianity as a proclamation of hope and life. Life is victorious over death, and the shackles that bind us in all sorts of deadly enslavements are broken by the risen liberator. Death is undone; and the words of Hosea, recited in triumph by Paul and set to music so stirringly by George Frederic Handel, continue to inspire us with hope and confidence:

> Death is swallowed up in victory.
> O death, where is your victory?
> O death, where is your sting?

Several fine books and articles are available on the resurrection. Among the more recent works are the following: Norman Perrin, *The Resurrection According to Matthew, Mark, and Luke* (Philadelphia: Fortress, 1977), published shortly after his death; my book *The Letter of Peter to Philip* (Chico, Calif.: Scholars, 1981), especially pp. 105–13; and James M. Robinson, "Jesus: From Easter to Valentinus (or to the Apostles' Creed)," *Journal of Biblical Literature* 101 (1982): 5–37. The translations from the Treatise on Resurrection in this chapter are taken from Robinson and Meyer, *The Nag Hammadi Library in English* (San Francisco: Harper & Row, 1977). For an analysis of the accounts of the resurrection appearances on the Damascus road, see Charles W. Hedrick, "Paul's Conversion/Call: A Comparative Analysis of the Three Reports in Acts," *Journal of Biblical Literature* 100 (1981): 415–32.

Hans Conzelmann has two excellent books of great value for our understanding of the passages we have discussed in Luke-Acts and 1 Corinthians: *The Theology of St. Luke* (New York: Harper & Row, 1960); and *1 Corinthians* (Philadelphia: Fortress, 1975), a Hermeneia commentary.

EPILOGUE

IF one theme may be proposed as a précis for this book, it may be that emphatic statement of the Gospel of John: the Word becomes flesh. For John, and for countless theologians since him, the mystery of the Incarnation demands an affirmation of both the divine and the human natures of Jesus. Several church councils, from Nicea to Chalcedon, wrestled with this difficult issue, and believers are still attempting to comprehend it. The Word becomes flesh: God approaches us and calls us in Christ, yet this divine Word is recognized in the very human figure of Jesus of Nazareth.

The flesh of the Word is not, therefore, just any flesh, or even flesh in the abstract. It is precisely the flesh of Jesus, and thus first-century Palestinian flesh. Such has been clear, I trust, from these discussions. We have seen Jesus as a first-century Jewish person, an itinerant rabbi and faith-healer who announced the coming of the kingdom of God in a highly charged, apocalyptic setting. Jesus was a man of his time, and expressed himself in a manner appropriate to his day. To suggest otherwise, I would offer, is to yield to an insidious docetism.

But the Word becoming flesh may be understood in another manner as well. In the Old Testament we read, time after time, of the Word of the Lord coming to the prophets of Israel and Judah as they exhorted and admonished the people to turn to the ways of God. This dynamic way of describing prophetic inspiration is often applied to the character of the Bible, so that the Bible itself is described as the Word of God. Using such a description, we immediately see that the notion of the Word becoming flesh may also have significance for the nature of the New Testament Gospels. For if the Gospels become flesh, then they too must be seen as truly human; and so they have appeared in these eight chapters. The New Testament Gospels, with all their polemical language and diversity of presentation, are first-century documents written by Christians who formulated their beliefs and fashioned their portraits of Jesus in their own ways. The Gospels, to be sure, are united in their concern for the person of Jesus, and communicate the same basic message—that Jesus is Lord. Yet they flesh out their interpretations of Jesus according to the real questions that needed to be faced, and the result is a collection of Gospels with rich diversity and human vitality. To conclude otherwise, I would also submit, is to fall into a docetic view of the Bible as Word.

From a time and place far away, Jesus of Nazareth and the Gospels proclaiming him address us with a Word of hope and salvation. The Word remains an ancient Word, articulated in a foreign tongue with foreign forms of expression. Yet when we grapple and struggle with the Word, we hear it as an authentic summons to us today. The reign of God is near; repent, believe, live! To study this ancient Word, and to hearken to its ever-present call, is both our challenge and our joy.

INDEX OF
ANCIENT SOURCES